HISTORY HAS TONGUES

HISTORY HAS TONGUES

A Study of the Comparative Development of Ancient and Modern Civilizations

by

WILFRID WOLFENDALE

With a Foreword by
W. L. CUTTLE
Dean and Tutor of Downing College, Cambridge

"History has tongues
Has angels has guns—has saved has praised—
Today proclaims
Achievements of her exiles long returned"

STEPHEN SPENDER—"The Exiles."

LONDON
VICTOR GOLLANCZ LTD
1946

TO

MY MOTHER

CB
67
.W6
1946

PRINTED IN GREAT BRITAIN BY RICHARD CLAY AND COMPANY, LTD.,
BUNGAY, SUFFOLK

CONTENTS

FOREWORD

This is a book by a prisoner of war. Its writer was a pupil of mine at Cambridge about sixteen years ago. He took his degree in Classics, but did not follow an academic or scholastic career: he went into business. He learned to know men and things, and saw something of foreign lands. Shortly before the war, he fore-armed himself: he joined the Territorial Army; and he was at Dunkirk as an officer in the Royal Artillery. After I had heard of his capture there, we had, within the imposed limits, an interesting exchange of letters. He was then in Oflag VI B, notorious for its overcrowding and bad conditions. Thence, in April 1942, he wrote to me that he had found a fellow-prisoner who had been a much more recent pupil of mine; and, under the leadership of the Chaplain of a Cambridge college, who had set up, at first entirely without books, a "university" with various "faculties", these two had lectured on ancient history. Lieut. Wolfendale confined himself (he said) to trends and tendencies; his colleague, with a much more recent experience of examinations, filled in the details. Thus Lieut. Wolfendale found in a return to his studies a sustaining force during all that time. The Red Cross sent books in increasing numbers, until there was a very useful library. Lieut. Wolfendale was enabled to develop his ideas and extend the scope of his inquiry. The result is this book. It was written wholly in a prisoners-of-war camp (in Oflag VII B), and it has not, I believe, been altered in any material sense since. Nor have the conclusions which the author drew during his long waiting—the means by which, if we interpret history aright, he hopes we may become "Good, great and joyous, beautiful and free"—been modified to suit the events which have occurred since he wrote them, in the summer of 1944. This is, I think, as it should be: this is a study conceived and born in a prisoners-of-war camp. That is, in a large measure, its significance. It is well—it is perhaps essential—that we should try to understand what passed in the minds of those who had that life. Too few of us in the world of today have time to sit down and think. A prolonged convalescence after illness might afford a man an opportunity for arranging his thoughts; but few of us would choose to have that costly opportunity. Still less, captivity; yet stone walls and iron bars saw the birth of Sir Walter Ralegh's *History of the World*, and Bunyan's *Pilgrim's Progress*, to name but two examples: and Mr. Charles Morgan made the concept of a scholar-soldier's using his internment as an opportunity for returning to his books and working out his ideas the theme of a novel: though his Lewis Alison worked under far different conditions from those of Oflag VI B. When Plato speaks of the "return to the Cave" which is necessary for the attainment of political insight, he says that when young we "treat argument [I quote from F. M. Cornford's translation of *The Republic*] as a form of sport solely for the purposes of contradiction". We are like puppies, enjoying the game. And so "after a long course of proving others wrong and being proved wrong themselves", young men "rush to the conclusion that all they once believed is false; and the result is that in the eyes of the world they discredit, not themselves only, but the whole business of philosophy". Hence, Plato says, "they must be sent down again into that Cave we spoke of and be compelled to take military commands and other offices suitable to the young, so that they may not be behind their fellow citizens in experience". And if they come through this test rightly, they will be fitted to "lift up the eye of the soul to gaze on that which sheds light on all things; and when they have seen the Good itself, take it as a pattern for the right ordering of the state and of the individual, themselves included".

Moral conclusions and general "laws" are not to be drawn from History without grave reservations and much heart-searching. But we owe it to those who in their years of great tribulation "thought on these things" to read what they thought, and to weigh it carefully. For it is an elixir compounded of our natural grossnesses and the subtler essences derived from study and reflection, and filtered through a mesh whose cost was greater than most of us would care to pay.

WILLIAM L. CUTTLE

Downing College, Cambridge,
May, 1946

PREFACE

This study will doubtless seem more remarkable for its omissions than for its contents. A survey of ancient civilization that takes no account of slavery, for example, and of modern which ignores female emancipation, can in no way claim to be synoptic, far less exhaustive; but the first consideration has been to be brief, and the second to be typical. The aim has been to bring to light the personal, underlying motives which have been responsible for the triumphs and achievements, and the personal shortcomings which have made inevitable the failures, and not to produce a full-scale history, which would be as far beyond the powers of the author as it would be outside the scope of such a volume.

TABLE OF EVENTS

CHAPTER I

INTRODUCTION

I

IT IS a common saying that History repeats itself, but it is not so common to pursue its similarities and dissimilarities far enough as to arrive at an estimate of what might be, as well as a recognition of what has been. We are more ready to view with complacence the repetitions that have occurred, whether they be to our advantage or not, than to avoid the recognizable mistakes of the past, and we undertake the reading of history more often from a desire for entertainment or from reasons of patriotism than with the intention of profiting from the achievements and failures of our ancestors in situations comparable to those of our own lifetimes. True it is, to a large degree, that history, like poetry, "only instructs as it delights", but nevertheless the delight should not be to the exclusion of a sense of its teaching, and an imaginative reconstruction in the light of later developments will often also increase the delight.

One of the obstacles to a proper appreciation of the values of history is the difficulty of recognizing the tendencies of our own era. We are prone to allow ourselves to be startled by the apparent suddenness of events in our own day, because we have not followed the sequence of less evident causes that have led up to them. For we are too close to our own times, too involved in the passions and prejudices of daily life, to see things broadly and in their right perspective, and we cannot distinguish the permanent from the merely ephemeral, the important from the trivial. It is not till we look back or are arrested by an event of more than usual magnitude that we realize that a chain of incidents has gone before, which has given the present the semblance of necessity or inevitability. At the moments of their happening, more often than not we overlook the bearing and direction of the facts around us, and the broad trends of life are generally invisible to us in the welter of minor details which seem to have more immediate significance.

With the past, it is the converse that is true. Only events of major importance pass into history, and the trivial, because of their very insignificance, are forgotten. We have handed down to us a broad outline of widely significant occurrences, punctuated by the high-spots which are the turning-points of history, so that the bearing of one event upon another becomes plain for all to see. The various causes that have contributed to a given effect render themselves obvious, and it needs no reference to abstruse logic or analytical genius to perceive the forces at work in any particular epoch.

The comparison of past and present is thus complicated by the difficulty of deciding what to compare, the one being a dry skeleton of inanimate bones, the other a living thing with all the movement and moodiness of body and soul. Just as the individual, with all his many sides, finds it difficult to say which is the real "ego", so, among all the conflicting currents of today, it is difficult to discover the main tendencies of our own times; and in proportion as it is hard to elucidate these tendencies, so is it hazardous to assert the comparableness of past situations, which might give a clue to the possible outcome of the present. The way of the psycho-analyst with the individual, however, must be the way of the historian with events, and an analysis of antecedents will generally bring to light the direction of a moment just as adequately as an analysis of an individual's life and thoughts will elucidate his character. Once the vital features of the present have been laid bare, the discovery of a comparable earlier situation becomes practicable.

It will thus be observed that the study of history subserves two complementary functions: the first, to show us, by a consideration of events leading up to our own day, the direction in which we are moving at the moment, including the significance of certain factors in our own lives; and the second, to compare the present situation—that is, the stage of development we have now reached—with a similar situation in an earlier development, so that we can see its implications and be guided by its advantages and defects in our dealings for the future. Needless to say, in the second aspect history never quite repeats itself, and there will always be certain factors present in the later situation that did not exist in the earlier, and vice versa, but there will be sufficient similarities, if the choice of situations is a good one, to make the effort both an interesting and a profitable occupation.

In both these functions of history—the analysis of the present and the comparison with the past—the immediate essential shows itself to be one of simplification. As our knowledge of the past is confined to the broad outline of events, a serviceable comparison will demand that our view of the present be reduced to a similar proportion. We must attempt to put the present into the same perspective as that of our historical survey, so that the two can be placed side by side for purposes of evaluation. But at the same time we must simplify our reading of the past, freeing it of those temporal trappings which belong solely to the period under review, and accentuate the underlying themes of permanent human value to which the details of mere material development are purely incidental. In this manner extremely simple pictures both of past and present will emerge, with large flat surfaces and none of the shading and intricate detail that are the attractions of biographical portraiture, but they will be arresting for the similarity of their broad patterning and the very sameness of their emotional colour.

With the provision of these two pictures, the function of history strictly is complete, and it is no part of the historian to carry the comparison to the lengths of forecasting the future; but the individual for his own interest is at liberty to pursue the story of the past beyond the point at which it is similar to events of the present day, and so conjecture on the possibility or otherwise of the pattern being repeated to its ultimate conclusion. From the knowledge of how an earlier generation attempted to cope with a situation identical in many respects with that of today, he may obtain some guidance as to what are likely to be the results of certain actions if taken in the present circumstances, and what are the pitfalls that must be avoided if earlier failures are not to be repeated.

2

The following chapters are an exercise in this kind of analysis, and the ambition is to compare no less than one complete civilization with another. Apart from the importance which naturally attaches to the events of our own lifetimes, there are many grounds for supposing that the present moment is a turning-point not only in the history of our country, but also in that of our civilization. The events of the past thirty years have been so tremendous, and their repercussions so far-reaching, that all our values and modes of existence have suffered a reversal. The very basis of our way of living both at home and abroad has been subverted with a completeness that renders the word "revolution" utterly powerless to describe it. Its ramifications extend into all the spheres of domestic, social, political, economic, psychological and religious life, even into time and space. In fact, the adaptability of the human being makes it almost impossible to appreciate adequately just how conclusively we have been uprooted within our generation, and unless we stop for a moment in our headlong rush, we do not realize that to pass from 1914 to 1944 is to bridge the gap from one world to another. Nor does a bewildering mass of legislation and treaty-making, both actual and proposed, or a constant stream of new inventions give us reason to believe that the process of change is in any way complete, or even nearing its end. The path of time is still far from clear.

One fact, however, emerges from the confusion, and that is that the process of change has itself undergone a change. There is a growing consciousness, however tardy it may be, that the idea of a return to the past is a figment of the imagination, a piece of wishful thinking, and that salvation lies in planning for the future construction of a new order of things rather than in a return to the old. The past thirty years have been the disintegration of an old world; the next thirty must be the building of a new: and whereas up to 1939 we tried to patch up a broken system, our disastrous failure means we must turn to the task of finding a fresh one. It is in this sense, then, that our civilization may be said to have reached a turning-point, and for this reason that we may be tempted to enquire whither we are heading and what sort of life we are laying up for ourselves in the future.

As has been indicated, however, to pick out those features of this present situation which have permanent importance, and separate them from the confused mass of events which have merely temporary value, is no easy task, and we are all of us more likely to have time and thought for the details of ordinary day-to-day existence than for the main lines of our general progress, which seem to be followed in spite of us. The method of selecting them that has been mentioned above is to trace the development of our civilization in broad outline from its very beginnings, and so arrive at a conceptual picture of what constitute the basic factors in our present stage of that development. This will eliminate those incidental accretions that assume a greater relative importance to us by reason of their closeness, and provide us with the bare skeleton stripped

14

of the flesh and blood that give it its baffling mobility. This method has been chosen for the following chapters.

Side by side with this analysis will be set the parallel development of an earlier civilization, the ancient world of the Greeks and Romans. This also will be in its broadest outlines, and will help to focus our attention on the salient features of our own and illuminate the significance of much that is obscure today. By the very lack of material progress and the absence of mechanical invention, the civilization of the ancients was itself infinitely less complex than ours, but when viewed over the distance of two thousand years its own lesser complexities smooth out into the simple pattern that makes it readily assimilable and ideal for the present purposes. Nor does the greater simplicity of the earlier era mean that it is not comparable with the modern world; for the main motives and springs of action hold good for all human beings, whatever their nationality or age. The habits and customs, the technique and appliances which time changes, leave their mark only on the outward lives and superficial organization of the people, and hardly affect the ultimate aims and aspirations which in the last resort mould the progress of mankind. The desire for material comfort, for social security and economic advancement is the same in all ages whatever the media in which that desire is expressed; while the conflict of ideologies, the lawless lusts of stronger wills and the painful birth of new moralities create the same havoc in the established order of the years before Christ as in the 20th century of His era.

To prove this equation is to be the object of the following chapters, and they will then proceed a step further and by a consideration of the later stages of the Roman Republic attempt to draw some conclusions about the probable progress of our own civilization if it follows the lines on which it is at present running.

3

As a preliminary it will be convenient to define quite broadly what we mean by civilization. It is a term we are apt to use freely enough, but often without any explicit views on its real implications, and if we are to arrive at any definite conclusions about either the ancient or the modern world, it is of the utmost importance that we have a clear conception of the thing we intend to discuss.

The readiest clue to its meaning is to be found in its logical antithesis to the word "barbarism", and though the mere verbal play of declaring what it is not is unlikely to conduce to satisfactory results, it does at least put us on the track of certain positive characteristics which are "of the essence". The chief aspect of what we mean by barbarism is its chaos or anarchy, and it is safe to say that a state of civilization primarily connotes the opposite of this—that is, order and discipline. It purports that the action of man has ceased to be a haphazard movement without regard to his fellows or environment, and that his efforts are canalized according to a definite pattern. Furthermore, barbarism implies the total lack of what we understand by organization, and so the society representing civilization must necessarily be organized beyond the primitive stage of the family or clan into a group of more complex relationships. There will be a co-ordination of effort along the lines of the established pattern for reasons other than mere kinship.

It will be noted that the description that has so far emerged would hold equally good of a beehive or an anthill, and we must take another implication from barbarism to lead us to the distinguishing feature of human society. For by the ascription of the term "barbarous" we mean also something that outrages what we call our finer feelings, and civilization must somehow be compatible with these more spiritual aspirations. It intends a stage of human development in which moral, æsthetic and intellectual values have come to have a distinctive place, and the previously mentioned co-ordination of effort has more than a purely utilitarian basis.

We can say, then, that civilized society is a group of human beings organized both for their spiritual and material advantage, and the degree of civilization is the greater or less according as the organization conduces to the greater or lesser advantage of its members, both spiritually and materially. This is a very rough and vague definition, and has no reference to the special features of our own or Græco-Roman civilization, but it will serve for the moment to keep our attention fixed on the salient points whilst we explore the enormous ramifications of this huge generalization.

We can now consider ourselves adequately equipped to make a start on our investigation. The method that will be adopted will be to analyse selected periods of ancient and modern history in turn, so that the correspondence of the two civilizations can be considered progressively, and then, when a point has been reached in the ancient world which corresponds to the present stage of the modern, we can go on to conjecture what a further correspondence would be likely to hold in store for us. We will begin at the beginning in both cases, and review first the rise of ancient Athens, and follow that immediately with an analysis of the Renaissance in Italy.

CHAPTER II

ANCIENT ATHENS

I

THE ANCESTORS of the people who were to be known to later ages as the Greeks were a northern people, a branch of the great Aryan family of which we ourselves are a part. They came from the hinterland of the European continent in the successive waves that characterize the migrations of uncivilized tribes, and settled in the Balkan Peninsula during the 15th to 10th centuries B.C. As the common heritage of their tall, fair-skinned race, they brought with them certain instincts which differentiated them from the indigenous, small, dark people they almost submerged in their new home, and these were to condition for always the progress of their subsequent development. These instincts are important, as they have survived and impregnated Western civilization up to the present day, and they are likely to tell us something of the underlying motives of history. Nowhere are they better exemplified than in the two monuments of Epic poetry, the "Iliad" and the "Odyssey", attributed to Homer about 900 B.C., which show us a people possessing in their maturer years all the feelings and attitudes that we usually associate with boyhood. For that reason they make their characters plain and easily read.

The first thing that strikes us about them is their robust healthiness, both of mind and body. They take pride in their physical prowess, and their mental outlook is what we term sane and natural. There is no undue emphasis on the ascetic, the morbid or the tortuous, and apart from a little boyish superstition, they are fearless both in life and death. Consonant with this ingenuousness are their plainness of speech and independence of spirit, and their ideal of a man is clearly one who speaks his mind and, accepting no one as his master,

17

has the resource to fend for himself. For all that, there emerges from time to time the germ of that spirit of compromise or reasonableness which lends itself to co-operation and discipline without the more pressing incentive of *force majeure*; and though they have all boyhood's ruthlessness and cruelty, the motive of pity is not absent. Startling, too, by its very brilliance is the strength of their imaginative vigour. If imagination is the prerogative of childhood, then these men were very infant prodigies. Both their invention and their facility of expression mark them as genuinely creative, giving point to a keen and sensitive observation of nature. Their main deficiency, as we view things today, is a religion. A moral standard of a sort they certainly possessed and a pantheon of gods, but they had nothing that even faintly resembles a religious awe of the divine or an explicit recognition of the mystical element in man.

We may sum up the basic character of the Greek race, then, as a proud self-sufficiency, tempered by an imaginative vision than can sometimes see the other man's point of view; and the history of Greece is the attempt of a people with this character to build a world to suit them.

2

The most tremendous results accrued from the arrival of this northern race in the warm Mediterranean basin, where climate and topography alike provided them with the most favourable conditions. They thrived at once, and after a few centuries of steady growth, blossomed with the triumphs of the 5th and 4th centuries B.C. which are our special concern in this chapter. Although the whole of Greece, including its colonies in Asia Minor, Sicily and the foot of Italy, shared in this achievement, it was the individual city of Athens that made the crowning effort and gave an inspiring lead in one sphere after another during those two eventful centuries; and it is to Athens in particular that we look for a supreme representation of both the glories and the shortcomings of Greek civilization as a whole.

To account for this difference of one small part from the whole, it is necessary to note a special feature of Greek development which held good till the 4th century B.C., and that is that the proud spirit of independence we have already observed, combined with the geographical conditions of the country to keep the inhabitants of the many narrow valleys politically, and to some extent culturally, distinct from each other. It was possible for the people of Attica—that is, the

18

immediate environs of the local metropolis of Athens—to create their own separate atmosphere, which nevertheless typifies, whilst at the same time excelling, the other local units or city-states of Greece.

In the year 510 B.C. Athens was just one of a conglomeration of small autonomous towns which accepted the idea of their racial affinity but recognized no political or economic union. In that year there occurred an event which was destined to have far-reaching repercussions on Athenian history. A local magnate whose father had half a century earlier established a mild autocracy, was assassinated by a well-timed conspiracy, and the citizens had need to consider what sort of government they were going to establish in its place. It gave an opportunity for a discussion of their personal and civic aims, and political theory which had been born a short time earlier took its first step forward. It had already been recognized that the congregation of people in a town was necessary for their better defence and organization, and that successful urbanization was rendered possible only by a surrender of some aspects of the individual's sovereignty, these concessions being regularized by the formulation of legal codes; but the fifty years' experience of despotism had now crystallized their views about those concessions, and a definite attempt was made to frame a constitution in which the liberty of the individual would be restored as completely as was consonant with the discipline that corporate living implied. Hence was evolved the first effective democracy, a polity which gave the maximum length of rein to the personal spirit of independence and an equal voice in the management of the combined resources.

Its details were soon worked out. The system of government by representation was still unknown, and matters of civic importance were decided by an assembly of the whole body of citizens. The civil magistracies, which were at first elective, were filled eventually by lot and made tenable for one year only. An original property qualification for full citizenship was steadily reduced, until by 452 B.C. the working-classes were the political equals of their social superiors, and the offices of State to which all were admitted were paid as a compensation for lost employment. The only officials exempt from this rapid democratization were the commanders of the military forces, who for obvious reasons had to be carefully selected and granted a more enduring term of service, and who by contrast acquired a prestige and influence extending far beyond a purely military sphere. The generals, in fact, became politicians, and by virtue of their responsibilities and experience were the effective leaders of the government.

When the Athenians considered this achievement, they were filled with pride and patriotism, and when the redoubled zeal with which they applied themselves to their business, and especially to their defence against oriental aggression, brought them quite unimagined success, they felt sure they had discovered the panacea for all ills. Their arms prospered throughout the Levant; their merchandise streamed out to all corners of the Mediterranean; riches poured in on them; and a public works programme bore visible witness to their prosperity with buildings and statuary of permanent interest. The city defences were rebuilt, and the harbour facilities of the Piræus were completely modernized. From a mainly agricultural community, Athens grew in half a century to be the greatest naval and mercantile Power of the Mediterranean, with important interests stretching from the Crimea to the Straits of Gibraltar. Nor were the achievements in the realm of art less impressive. Apart from the architecture and sculpture already noted, painting reached a new level of technical and artistic excellence: poetic drama was carried to heights that only Shakespeare has surpassed; and more than a beginning was made in scientific speculation, history and philosophy. The justification of democracy seemed complete.

In point of fact, it was too complete. The more conservative neighbouring cities could not but view this phenomenal expansion with fear and envy, and the policy of the Athenians themselves did nothing to reassure them. For their genuine pride gave place to arrogance, and their commercial supremacy was relentlessly transformed into an out-and-out empire. The opposition slowly gathered strength, until at last in 431 B.C. Athens was drawn into open war with a powerful alliance under the leadership of Sparta, a reactionary, totalitarian State in Southern Greece. There followed a long and fluctuating struggle in which she was gradually brought to her knees, and the dream of democratic imperialism vanished in the humiliations of unconditional surrender in 404 B.C. With it passed also extreme democracy. It gave place in the next century to a more moderate but more acceptable version of it; but though Athens still had immense contributions to make by pouring her remaining vigour into the more reflective pursuits of philosophy, science, literature and the arts, the old impetus was gone. When the Greek right to political disunity was finally broken at the battle of Chæronea in 338 B.C., Athens passed under the yoke of Macedon with little more ado than a display of Demosthenic oratory.

3

After the *débâcle* of 404 B.C. the Athenians themselves were led to enquire into the reasons for their collapse, and the leading philosophical schools, those of Plato and Aristotle, came to throw the blame on inherent defects in radical democracy itself. In a constitution where every man's vote was of equal weight, the decision automatically lay with the less educated working-classes, who were in a big majority, but who could not be expected to have the experience, or the sense of responsibility begotten of experience, necessary to cope with the business of State. All would be well so long as a Pericles was at the helm with the ability to "put over" wise counsel, but in the absence of such leadership the direction of affairs inevitably fell to the readiest tongue that could whip up the passions and prejudices of the mob and peddle a policy with the greatest popular appeal, regardless of prudence. In this way, demagogy, pandering to a reckless lust for power, had brought about the worst excesses of Athenian imperialism and precipitated Athenian arms into the follies of wild-cat strategy. Worse than this, there had followed a lamentable decay in public morale and integrity which had destroyed the very foundations of internal security. Plato himself concluded from this that the natural inequality of man rendered democracy an impracticable vision, and for his own ideal republic he plumped for a strict authoritarianism which would keep the business of government firmly in the hands of men equipped for the task both by nature and training.

But, as Plato realized, there was more in it than just that. There was obviously something very right, just as much as there was something very wrong, about a way of life that could produce the artistic triumphs of 5th-century Athens, and though Plato's political experiences made him distrust the emotions, he was too sensitive himself not to realize the heights to which they could aspire if properly directed, and the essential part they played in the constitution of the "good life". The spiritual side of man, he knew, must be catered for as well as the material, and this the early democracy had clearly done to perfection. Plato's diagnosis of this situation was that "love" was the moving force—love of home, of the city, the common weal and the body of fellow-citizens—and in his "Republic" he sought to inculcate this spirit of patriotism in all grades of society by propaganda and education.

This reading, however, is not wholly adequate, as it takes no account of the incentive to individual effort that came with the discovery of free self-expression. Although the whole Ægæan world was at this time seething with intellectual speculation, it was Athenian political liberty, despite its occasional lapses, that gave it the kindliest home and brought it to its noblest fulfilment. The opportunity there presented for personal advancement was not lost on the Greeks, with their instinctive leaning towards self-sufficiency, and although temporarily at least there was a nice balance of individual and communal effort, and consciousness of the distinction was not fully alive, it is a false diagnosis to see nothing of the personal motive, even in the Olympian aloofness of a Pericles. Altruism is an even worse description of their attitude.

Nevertheless, it was a very different thing from what followed. The very speculation that was cherished speedily led to a frank recognition of the conceptual difference between the individual and communal motives, and the vague feeling that the glorification of Athens was the glorification of the Athenian, and vice versa, changed first to enlightened self-interest, and then to open and practised individualism. The results for political honesty were fatal, and, transferred also to the sphere of inter-State relations, produced the rank imperialism which was the chief mode of expression for the unenlightened and impecunious city-mob.

Two things alone could have prevented, or at any rate deferred, this degeneration, and Plato again saw them in part. The first was the education of the masses and the inculcation of a broad-mindedness that would have seen the only sure foundation for personal welfare in the common good, and kept their attitude at least on the plane of enlightened self-interest. But though Plato thus foreshadowed State socialism of education, in his version it was intended to be strictly vocational and directed solely to the goal of making the various classes contented with their lot. Only the few elect were to be allowed the advantages of a liberal education, and Plato's distaste for the proletariat did not permit him to envisage the possibility of any high general level of attainment or appreciation of the true values of life.

The other remedy would have been an awakening of the individual and social conscience to the ethical obligations imposed by human society and the consequent strengthening of the moral fibre. We have seen that the Greeks possessed little or no tradition for either public or private morality, and even what little there was, was swept away in the intellectual ferment of the 5th century. Having no religious background to their morality, they were particularly vulnerable tô this sort of attack; for when man's enquiring mind could find no deeper foundation for morality than his own unconsidered habit, he saw no *a priori* reason for disregarding the more attractive claims of his own passions. Thus, self-expression, and even self-gratification, became the only standards of virtue.

In this dilemma, it was Socrates' unique contribution to ethics that he formulated the idea of the conscience as a guide to conduct, and Plato, following his lead, took it over complete into his own philosophy, as the basis for his system of education. By teaching and training, the individual would be roused into permanent awareness of the dictates of conscience until it automatically imposed self-discipline and restraint. And if this was a world of men like Socrates and Plato, how admirable a solution! But whereas Socrates' will-power was such that to be convinced of the rightness of a thing was to act—and in that way for him knowledge *was* virtue—for us frailer mortals the choice is not so obvious nor the course of action so easy. Therein lies the great shortcoming of the Socratic doctrine. Morality requires a surer sanction and the will a more cogent spur than can ever be normally provided by the promptings of the individual conscience.

4

So far in this chapter the emphasis has fallen on the political aspect of Greek development, and indeed it was in that light that the Athenians themselves saw the problems of life in the 5th century. But just as our own criticism has tended to turn to their individual shortcomings, so did ancient investigation come to turn that way and face a growing realization that progress in politics was possible only according as the several members of the body politic were fitted for it. Better political organization would follow automatically from an improvement in the personal, and therefore national, character, and this was the chief lesson of the Athenian experiment in radical democracy. The conditions for intellectual and æsthetic activity had been perfect, but the sacrifice on the moral side had been ultimately devastating.

Now the great incentive to their activity in the field of the intellect and the senses had been a form of idealism. Their newly found liberty had given them the opportunity for expressing themselves in their own way, and that expression naturally took the form of their conscious and subconscious aspirations, which lay, as we have seen, in the direction of the reason and the body. They had certain concepts drawn from the world around them, in particular the ingenuity of man and his physical prowess, and their creative imaginations, working on these concepts, had projected what might be on what was. Hence came their ideals, and in proportion as they were emotionally coercive in the heat of discovery, so they produced results in the intellectual and æsthetic development of the Athenians. Hence too came that consciously idealistic atmosphere in their literature and art which attracts or repels us according as we ourselves are moved by a spirit of idealism or disillusionment.

Guided by considerations of this sort, Plato in his later years came to the conclusion that if this achievement had been combined with moral idealism as well, the subsequent decay of Athenian society might have been averted. Had the individual had some ideal of Goodness to which his conduct might have been directed, just as he had ideals of Truth and Beauty for the guidance of his powers of reason and his æsthetic appreciation, the few ethical standards of the day would not have fallen victim so easily to the process of rationalization. Further, he came to realize that though the Socratic doctrine of the conscience supplied a perfectly adequate machinery for the conveyance of moral teaching, it desperately needed a motor if it was to be made to work, and this motor he correctly saw in the emotional strength of idealism.

Out of his earlier views on patriotism, therefore, he formulated his intellectual idea of transcendental "Goodness", and intended that a love of this sublime idea should be an eternal inspiration to mankind in its pursuit of virtue. But there is a world of difference between the statement of a need and its satisfaction, and though this idea has lived on as a moral ideal which has stirred the imagination of men in all ages, it has failed utterly to come down to the level of ordinary life and supply the needs of common humanity. In other words, Plato was not Christ. But he does claim the world's gratitude as having been the first to see the necessity for some spiritual bond to unite the peoples of the earth in fellowship,

24

and as having raised a hymn of praise whose harmonies can still at times be heard above the din of total war.

5

These were the issues that were raised at the very outset of Græco-Roman civilization. A bold experiment had been made in the field of human liberty, based on a confident assumption of human perfection, and the results in certain directions had been stupendous. In art and literature a standard of taste and technique was set up that has acted as a spur to all succeeding ages, and an impulse was given to science and philosophy that opened new vistas of achievement to the imagination of mankind. But the Golden Age passed, and the whole structure was brought to the ground by an unforeseen deficiency in the make-up of man. His moral attainment was found to lag far behind the stage of his intellectual development, and the brilliant promise of his art was nullified by his inability to live in harmony with his fellows.

The sense of disappointment and disillusionment that followed was so intense as to affect the whole course of Greek civilization, and never again were the Greeks prepared to take the risk of freedom and equality, owing to fear of its dismal consequences. They chose instead the safer course of limited objectives and comfort, and so suffered the mediocrity, that we shall see in the kingdoms of the Hellenistic Age.

CHAPTER III

THE RENAISSANCE IN ITALY

I

HAVING TRACED the beginning of things in Greece, we will now turn to the modern world and see how our own civilization began. For this we must look to Italy. When the Roman Empire finally collapsed in the early 5th century A.D., the countries of Western Europe were laid open to a vast inrush of barbarian peoples who had been hammering for years and with ever-increasing violence on the frontiers of the North, and who were now free to surge wherever the prospect of plunder impelled them. Northmen and Saxons swept across the North Sea into England; Franks poured into France; and Italy received a flood of Lombards, Goths and Visigoths. The new-comers were nearly all of the Aryan race, another branch of which had invaded the Balkans two thousand years earlier, and they submerged the old inhabitants almost as completely as their ancestors had done in the previous age. With the long period of their acclimatization and settling down to new homes, known to history as the Middle Ages, we are not here concerned, any more than we were with the Greeks between the 15th and 5th centuries B.C., and we are only interested to consider them as a guide to the basic character of that people of Italy who were to open up the drama of the modern world.

For this purpose we will again turn to the most famous poet of the age, and one who with Homer and Milton makes a triad of the world's most famous epic poets, Dante Alighieri. Beneath the idealizations of his poetry we get the impression of a proud, self-conscious race, mercurial, perhaps, from genera-tions of residence in the Mediterranean, but swift to the defence of its preconceived rights and brave to the point of fool-hardiness. The verse itself shows an unsurpassable appreciation of the power and music of language, and its imaginative strength is such as to leave the mind gasping.

In one major respect, however, it differs totally from the epics of Homer, and that is its Christian theme, background and inspiration. These give the poetry of Dante a moral fer-vour and a religious devoutness wholly alien to the pagan directness of Homer. At this point it is necessary to consider briefly what had been the chief results of the advent of Christianity and how it had affected the development of men's thought. The Christian doctrine had opened to men the path of moral idealism which Plato had sought to tread, and supplied in the person and teaching of Christ a moral ideal inestimably more effective than Plato's intellectual idea. But it had done more than that. By the divinity of His person, Christ had linked to morality the sanction of religion, and thereby given it the inspiring strength of devotional exercise. The spirit of love, which in Platonic theory had been a thing of the mind, accessible only to abstract contemplation, now became actual in the lives of men and women, and made itself personal and comprehensible in the simple story of the gospels. The idea of brotherly love became a commonplace of thought, if less actual in fact.

The spread of such a doctrine could only work for the betterment of mankind, and did indeed bring about a revolu-tion in manners. It played a large part in civilizing the Germanic hordes of Western Europe, and set a new standard of decency in both private and public morals. But in considering the period of the later Middle Ages we must rid our minds of any preconceived ideas we may have about Christianity drawn from our own experiences. The fact was that in the 13th and 14th centuries, particularly in the Italy of Dante and Petrarch, the pure flame of Christianity was burning very low indeed. Despite the heights of religious fervour to which a Thomas Aquinas or a Dante could rise, the Christianity of the times was divided between a sterile scholasticism on the one hand, and a rank superstition on the other. The monks of Christendom had spent centuries performing mental acrobatics in pursuit of their own tails, and their outmoded metaphysical speculation had drawn the higher theology of the Church out of all contact with reality. In these circumstances, the needs of the masses had been left to take care of themselves, and the creed of love had gradually changed to one of such superstitious fear that the person of Christ, the very incarnation of lovingkindness, became a figure of awe and ferocity requiring the intercession not only of the Virgin Mary, but also of a whole circus of blessed saints, angels and archangels.

The Latin races have always tended to be pagan, and the mediæval Italians were no exception. Despite the superficially softening effects of Christianity, therefore, we may sum up our broad analysis of their character as not unlike that of the pre-classical Greeks.

2

Politically, at this time, Italy was considered to be a part of the Holy Roman Empire, a connection which had had, and was still to have, the most calamitous effects on Italian history. For the idea of the Holy Roman Empire was a fatal hallucination clung to with all the desperate strength that German pigheadedness and ecclesiastical bigotry could muster, and doomed to drag down with it all that it obsessed to the hell of unending strife and disruption. As a survival, it was interesting, as an instrument of present policy, it was deadly; and long after the West and North of Europe had broken away from the crumbling structure that was once the realm of Charlemagne, the tattered Emperors in Germany on the one side and the Hildebrandine Popes on the other poured out the resources of central and southern Europe in an endeavour to keep Germany and Italy bound in the ramshackle machinery of a worn-out feudalism, with consequences for both as disastrous as the Axis of a later day.

In Italy, loyalty to Church and Empire fought with each other in the feuds of the Guelphs and the Ghibellines, and unification of the country was impossible. Only gradually did repugnance of German domination combine with despair of Papal leadership to overcome the chimæra of German- or Papal-led Christian unity, and then in such a way that it rested upon individual cities to win their own independence and carve out the means of their own separate existence. By the 13th and 14th centuries, therefore, Italy presented much the appearance of classical Greece, with a conglomeration of autonomous city-states, paying lip-service, indeed, to the Emperor over the Alps or the Pope, but in reality accepting no union either with the Empire or with each other. Florence, Venice, Genoa, Pisa and the like were the political descendants of Athens, Corinth, Argos and Sparta, and only in the far South did the kingdom of Naples and Sicily possess an extent of territory greater than that of a small English county.

Now, in striking for their independence, the cities of Italy were making more than a political gesture: they were breaking with a way of life. For the Holy Roman Empire was the crowning edifice of a vast social organization that covered the whole range of human society and directed the whole course of mediæval civilization. This was the system of Feudalism which was universal in Europe; for though France and England had broken away from the main stock, it was only to form their own private systems on the model of the central organization. This system was built up on the idea of corporate existence, each member of society being wholly dependent on, and sub-servient to, a member of a higher level of society, in a scale ascending from the humblest serf who tilled the ground, up through the grades of yeomen, lords of the manor, shire-lords, dukes and kings, to the figure of the Emperor, sitting in majesty at the summit of the pyramid. It catered in advance for everyone's needs, and everything in life was fixed, in-evitably and eternally. Changes in occupation, social status or habitat were barred, and in theory even the actual course of men's thoughts was dictated from above.

The action of a single city, therefore, in going its own way and establishing its own republican institutions struck to the very heart of the feudal idea, and opened up the way to an entirely new mode of living. Nor were the results long in making themselves apparent: for the advent of freedom, both political and social, reacted on the peoples of northern Italy in a manner that is equalled only by the story of classical Greece. First came an increase in wealth and a rise in the standard of living; for the abolition of feudal dependence and repression gave the artisan classes a new incentive for their work which both increased production and stimulated the demand. Trade and commerce began to thrive, first internally, then between cities, and finally overseas, until by the middle of the 14th century huge fleets were going out from Venice, Genoa and Pisa which dominated the Mediterranean and brought to Italy all the wondrous wares of the East. At the same time, the sense of being pioneers in an alien world made them look to their own defence, and heightened both the necessity and the zest for guarding the rewards of their hard-won liberty. A spirit of intense patriotism informed their every move.

More fateful still for Europe was the revival of learning that followed. Italy was rich everywhere with the crumbling remains of the Roman Empire to which tradition assigned the romance of a Golden Age, but which for centuries had been ignored except as handy quarries for material. These were now viewed with new eyes by a people who found the crude, irrational methods of feudalism unsuited to their fresh commercial interests, who had to strike out new ways of coping with a thousand new problems, and who had been taught to believe that Roman civilization was perfection itself. Architecture was naturally the first thing to be studied, but sculpture, painting, literature, and medicine quickly followed suit, and zealous interest soon turned to active imitation.

The results of all these activities on the intellectual and æsthetic development of the republican Italian cities were profound. Their outlook ceased to be mediæval. Nevertheless it was not yet fully modern. In particular, a long experience of the feuds of the Guelphs and Ghibellines had accustomed them to turbulence in internal affairs which gave their party politics a rancour and ferocity fatal to democracy. As a result, during the hundred years between the middle of the 14th and middle of the 15th centuries the republics one by one despaired of obtaining the smooth conduct of affairs and continuity of policy essential for their new capitalistic ventures, and, having suspended their democratic constitutions, accepted ruling princes from among the rural baronies which had survived the breakdown of feudalism. The relationship between prince and people, however, was very different from that between baron and serfs, and there was a definite understanding by which the prince's sphere of authority was confined to civic administration and external policy, so as to allow the mercantile and trades elements a free hand with their business. Indeed, in some cases—as, for example, with the Medici at Florence—the princes were not taken from the old Knights of Chivalry at all, but were actual commercial families who had amassed huge private fortunes from their then world-wide connections.

We have now reached the peculiar feature of Renaissance Italy—a galaxy of independent cities, each a busy hive of industry and commerce, with the inhabitants free and secure to work out their own lives and livelihoods, in return for which they maintained in princely splendour a ruling house whose task it was to give efficient government in both external and internal affairs. Then in 1453 occurred an incident which more than any other single event determined the course of the Renaissance. The Turks broke into Constantinople, for more than eleven centuries the capital of the Eastern or Greek half of the old Roman Empire, and a flood of refugees poured into Italy, bringing with them all the forgotten store of ancient Greek culture. The Roman culture the Italians had already been studying was certainly derived from the Greek, but it was only a pale copy in itself, and moreover had been fantastically distorted beyond all recognition by the warped imaginations of the mediæval Schoolmen. But now the fresh breeze of Greek science, literature and art blew straight from the pages of Plato, the dramatists and historians, and the Greek virtue of direct and rational thinking returned to thrilling life. The impact left its mark at once, and the art and literature of Italy took the immense strides forward which brought it within fifty years to the glorious achievements of Leonardo da Vinci, Michelangelo, Raphael, Bramante, Ariosto and Tasso. No less did the success of rationalization show itself in material things, and a wave of prosperity, luxury and brilliance swept over the whole of north and central Italy. The courts of the princes became proverbial for magnificence, and the ordinary populations took as much delight in this sign of their civic excellence as in the betterment of their own domestic appurtenances.

All this display of wealth and opulence, however, attracted the greedy eyes of monarchs outside the bounds of Italy, and the Italians themselves brought the moment of their doom ever nearer by their own inter-city strife and embroilment. From the year 1494, when Ludovico Sforza, Duke of Milan, invited the French King to help him in his wars of aggression, Italy became a battle-ground, not only for Italians caught in the fatal lure of self-aggrandizement, but also for Frenchmen in search of conquest and loot, Germans pursuing the mirage of the Holy Roman Empire, and Spaniards who merely came to kill and repress. Cities were destroyed, and whole populations driven into the wilderness; Rome itself was stormed and sacked in 1527 with indescribable barbarity; and the conquering Turks were allowed to desolate up to the very lagoons of Venice. Not even as they writhed in the throes of indiscriminate invasion, were the Italians able to combine for their own relief, but blindly pursued their internecine contentions, heedless of the future; and only when the foreign kings were gorged with blood and worn out with plundering did Italy find a respite—the respite of exhaustion. By the terms of the Treaty of Cambray in 1530, northern Italy fell under the unfeeling heel of the Hapsburgs, where she lay writhing and powerless for three long centuries to come.

Nor was political impotence all. The laxity of the Vatican's direction of the Church of Rome, the immorality of its conduct and its blind pursuit of temporal power had alienated huge areas of Christendom, and gave rise eventually to the Lutheran Reformation, which not only halved the spiritual power of Rome at a blow, but also provoked the Catholic Counter-Reformation of 1545. This, in its inquisitorial demand for mediæval orthodoxy, had necessarily to apply the most stringent repressive measures on the artistic and scientific progress of its followers in Italy, and inexorably led to their intellectual and æsthetic emasculation. The Italian Renaissance was over.

3

The similarity of the broad outline of this story to that of ancient Greece is immediately obvious. In both cases a group of city-states win their way to autonomy and under the impulse of this movement create the conditions most favourable for their intense activity in practically all the spheres of human life; and then at the moment of their climax, falling victim to a chronic inability to co-operate, they are overtaken by disaster and collapse, yet leave behind a legacy that endows a civilization. In searching for the motive forces of the later story, therefore, we may let ourselves be guided by the results of our earlier survey, and indeed we shall again find that enthusiasm in pursuit of certain ideals is the deciding factor.

Just as political freedom in 510 B.C. was the starting-point of the Athenian rise to glory, so the impetus acquired in achieving Italian autonomy created the conditions for the subsequent triumphs.

As has already been pointed out, severance from the Holy Roman Empire was not merely political in its implications: it was a break with a civilization. The system of feudalism had imposed a regimen on all the functions of life, and abandoning it meant a sudden freedom from both mental and physical restraint. Instead of being compelled to conform to cramping pattern, everyone could follow his own bent and enjoy the fruits of his own labour, and human diversity was again allowed full freedom of expression. This movement gathered momentum from its very novelty. Now, the process of self-expression meant giving rein to their conscious and sub-conscious aspirations, and these aspirations, being formed from their judgments of actual experiences, naturally drew them first towards their various cities, the entities that offered them protection and a congenial home. The ideas of corporate living and patriotism were made to seem desirable in themselves, and success of the city meant success for the citizen and vice versa. This success, too, had to be made visible by the praise and ornamentation they lavished on it. Hence came the initial impulse.

Then, in the course of time, the various enterprises they undertook began to have values in and for themselves, and commerce, art and literature, gaining more relative importance, took the strides forward we have seen; and when at last, after 1453, Greek example suddenly gave them new standards of taste and technique, their enthusiasm and accomplishment simply leapt ahead. Greek idealism, seen through the eyes of 15th- and 16th-century Italy, irradiated the paintings of Raphael, as it did all but the latest sculptures of Michelangelo.

Just as the breakdown of feudalism gave new life to literature and art, so did it release new forces in the world of thought, and here, too, the Greek influence was decisive. A native curiosity had already begun to make men question and think for themselves—whereby the shallowness of scholasticism was soon exposed; and then, in the very moment when anti-quated authority was overthrown, Greek philosophy arrived to lend them its humanist ideals, which seemed the very wisdom of the ages. "Man is the measure of all things", declared Protagoras in 5th-century Athens; and man was

32

similarly the measure of all things for the Florentine circle of Lorenzo di Medici. This was the attitude that enabled the Italians to rid themselves of the imaginary "causes" postulated by a twisted Aristotelianism, and gave them that confidence in the powers of the human intellect which led to a rational investigation of cause and effect, and the birth of Science.

So far, however, we have looked only at one side of the picture: now we must turn to the other; and we find that just as it was a decay of moral idealism that brought Athens to disaster, so it was with Renaissance Italy. The story is repeated of an instinctive leaning to self-sufficiency being aggravated by the overthrow of external authority and turning to unrestrained expression of the individual personality. There thus came about the same lack of any inner regard for the obligations imposed by society. For to the Italian of the Renaissance not only was man the measure of all things, but every man was his own yard-stick, and he recognized no criteria in the conduct of his life but his own feelings and desires. Greek directness and Greek logic had taught them how to think and analyse, but Greek scepticism, with its emphasis on the human reason, made them overlook the need for the other values in life. Cold calculation took the place of ordinary human kindness, and the *beau ideal* of the age is summed up in the epithet it elicited—Macchiavellian.

In such a society there was no room for moral idealism, and such as there had been at the outset was quickly squeezed out. The better side of their patriotism was undermined from the start by the conflicting claims of Church and Empire, and we have seen how, quite early in their history, an inability to control the turbulent elements of their populace led to a suspension of their democratic institutions in favour of ruling princes. Their ambition for the progress of their cities was centred, not in the ideal of freedom itself or a fellow-feeling for their countrymen, but in the personal advancement and material benefits it brought with it.

Nor was a decadent Christianity able to supply anything of their need. The Church of Rome was both discredited and suspect, and its complete secularization in the last decades of the 15th century killed both its religious and moral authority. The Pope was just another temporal prince, with all the personal and political ambitions of a Sforza or a Medici, and the threats and fulminations of a Papal Bull had little more than a diplomatic effect. The mediæval devoutness was dead.

The consequences for Italy in a world of power-politics

could not be long delayed. The very wealth and culture they neglected all else to obtain were a lure to foreign aggression, and the perpetual wars in which they indulged were the occasion of foreign interference. Yet so deeply had the madness driven that they were unable to produce even the spirit of co-operation to oppose it. Instead, an insane reliance on their own city-defences made them rather welcome it, and the only leagues and confederacies they ever made were for the completer spoliation of other Italians.

4

We are now in a position to assess briefly the importance of the Italian Renaissance for modern Europe whose beginning it marked. Far and away the most momentous achievement was the breakdown of Feudalism and all that that implied. The world had been led back from the illogicality and disregard for human values that ruled the Gothic period, and reintroduced to the sane and the rational. Human reason was again allowed to assert itself against the mysticism and deliberate obscurantism of the Middle Ages. But more than this, an example had been given of what could be accomplished by it, and men could see in the realm of art and literature the rewards that awaited an unbounded enthusiasm for the humanist ideals of harmony and proportion. The classical value of unity in diversity had returned to mankind.

There had also returned the value of individual life. Men ceased to be cogs in a great machine that was powerless to move anyway, and became personalities with an independent existence. Society broadened to incorporate a huge mass of people who had hitherto been voiceless and submerged, and who were henceforward to play an increasing part in the business of life. For the moment, the impress of feudalism still lingered on in the sphere of politics, and except for a few abortive attempts at democracy, both in the beginning and later, men still had neither the competence nor the incentive to govern themselves. But though the tradition continued of a ruling caste which had the influence and experience for the task, nevertheless the path to political power was not entirely closed to the rest of mankind. Personality and single-mindedness could win through to high place, as we saw with the Medici at Florence, and the new relationship between ruler and ruled left opportunities for outstanding talent. Competitive, capitalist society had begun. The rulers, too, had left a high standard of magnificence and good taste, and their patronage of the arts, which had helped to produce the master-pieces of the age, was to be imitated for centuries.

The Renaissance in Italy, however, had also given a warning to men. The worst prognostications of outraged morality, both in Italy and abroad, were more than fulfilled by the disasters that eventually overcame this unbounded enthusiasm for the ideals of humanism, and the voices crying in the wilderness were justified in inveighing against the prevalence of self-sufficiency. The lack of external authority, whether of the Church or the Empire, to enforce the obligations to God and morality, was not in itself necessarily decisive; but when combined with a collapse of moral idealism, and consequently moral discipline, it proved fatal. Man's intellectual development was shown to be far in advance of his moral attainment, and a sense of caution for the future was one of the legacies for the rest of Europe.

5

We have now completed the first stage of our exercise, which was a comparative analysis of the beginning of ancient and modern civilization, and have found a close similarity not only in the motivating forces, the course of development and the "end of the beginning", but also in the values that gained currency and the things that were neglected. All these, of course, are only different aspects of the same two objects, but they may be separated conceptually for the purpose we have in view, and the progressive similarity we have elicited may be said to have justified it. We will therefore proceed to the next stage of the analysis, which deals with the period in which the new civilizations spread—the Hellenistic Age and the rise of nationalist Europe.

CHAPTER IV

THE HELLENISTIC AGE

I

DURING THE years 336 B.C. to 323 B.C. Alexander the Great accomplished one of the most impressive feats in all history. He carried the arms of Macedon and Greece victoriously over the whole of the Near and Middle East, and opened up

Asia Minor, the Levant, Egypt, Mesopotamia, Persia, Afghanistan and India as far as the Punjab, to the influence of Greek civilization. The effects on both Greeks and non-Greeks were naturally enormous, and our task is to sort out the most decisive. First, the outward political results.

It has already been observed that in 338 B.C., after the battle of Chæronea, Greece ceased to be independent and passed under the domination of Macedon. Macedon was a semi-Greek kingdom to the north of the peninsula, which had so far taken no part in the democratic and cultural development of Greece proper, but had recently been organized on the most up-to-date lines by Alexander's father, Philip II. The Greeks themselves still thought of the Macedonians as half-barbarians because they did not affect the political, scientific and artistic interests of the south, but the military power that Philip built up left them in no doubt as to what could be done by the application of Greek planning and organization to a backward race. Then, when Alexander the Great smashed country after country, it was obvious to everyone that centralization of authority in the hands of a single man, imbued with the powers of Greek scientific calculation, offered almost illimitable possibilities, and the prestige thus won by autocracy was decisive in subsequent politics, even apart from such doctrines of the divinity of kings as Alexander brought back with him from the East.

After the death of Alexander in 323 B.C. his newly-won empire was split up amongst his generals, and there arose over the Near East a constellation of petty kingdoms all aping the example of Macedon. Their military foundation, however, led to their continual embroilment, and after a series of wars and alliances, there emerged three major, dominant Powers who directed the chief course of events for the next century— Macedon itself, with a grip on the mainland of Greece, Syria, controlling the Levant and most of Asia Minor, and Egypt, in reality the Greek colony of Alexandria backed by the fabulous wealth and fecundity of the Nile Valley. The further eastern territories fell away almost immediately, and reverted to alien lands.

Meanwhile, a period of prosperity began such as the Eastern Mediterranean had never known before. The impulse to trade given by Alexander's conquests was immense, as whole countries were opened up to receive the products of Greek industry, and raw materials, carpets, silks and spices streamed back in exchange. Despite the continual wars of conquest, the standard of living rose steadily, and the benefits of Greek culture extended over a wider and wider area. Greeks themselves had followed in the wake of conquest and trade, and established flourishing colonies in all the towns of any size, and their language, being that of the government, soon became the *lingua franca* of the whole Near East. With it came Greek literature and Greek philosophy, which took root readily and produced fresh fruits in their new homes, whilst sculpture and architecture flourished abundantly, and the types of furniture, household utensils and clothes became standard everywhere. By 200 B.C. the traveller from Athens did not feel himself in an alien land whether he went to Brindisi or Benghazi, Alexandria or Alexandretta. In fact, everything was Greek, and everything prospered.

2

At this point we must re-define what we mean by "Greek". In the early chapter we surveyed the original fount of Greek civilization, which is generally called "Hellenic" (from "Hellas", the Greek name for Greece), but the form of it that was now current differed considerably, and is usually called "Hellenistic".

In Hellenic civilization we saw that everything centred round the development of political autonomy; whereas now the chief feature of political life was the kingdom or autocracy which gave the other no scope. The ideals of political liberty and independence that suffered such a setback in the fall of Athens had undergone a permanent eclipse, and except for a few debased survivals, or as objects of theoretical study, played no part in the life of the Hellenistic Age. Both conscious and subconscious aspirations had changed direction, therefore, and to understand the tendencies of the time we must examine their new objects of attachment.

We saw that the growth of individualism had been one of the chief contributory causes of the collapse of Athens, by undermining the patriotism and spirit of co-operation that had been its original mainstay, and that the individual had set more store by his own personal welfare than that of the political unit of which he was a member. This spirit everywhere was cumulative in its effects; for as the willingness of the people to exert themselves for their country declined, there was a proportionate decline in their country's power to protect itself and its liberties, and when their country finally lost its independence to one of the major kingdoms, they gave up not only the will to assert themselves, but also the power. They were thus driven to apply themselves to their personal interests as much by circumstances they had themselves created as by their inclination; and commerce and industry supplied the place of priority that had formerly belonged to political and civic business—how successfully, their prosperity has already testified.

Along with their passion for politics died the internal rancour and dissension it had bred, as also their desire for war-like adventure. The continuous wars we have seen in the previous section were purely the affair of kings in search of conquest and aggrandisement, and the armies they used were almost wholly comprised of mercenaries drawn from non-Greek as well as Greek sources. The ordinary citizen was little affected by them, save in so far as his taxes increased or decreased with the fluctuating fortunes of his king, and he pursued his career uninterrupted by events which had merely dynastic importance. This meant that the chief cause of their inability to live together in harmony was practically eliminated.

Moreover, they had not lost sight of the lesson of the Athenian downfall, in which a blind pursuit of individualism had led to the ruin not only of an empire, but also of the private citizens involved in it, and it was realized that the furtherance of personal interest to the exclusion of all regard for the future simply did not pay. Social virtues, therefore, came to have place and meaning, and the good manners that symbolize them revolutionized the outward appearance of society. Commerce and industry, too, meant co-operation and a measure of honesty, and in general a broad-minded cosmopolitanism took the place of the former parochial intenseness.

In this situation there were naturally ample means and leisure for the amenities of that culture which was part of the Greek inheritance and pride, and a growing output of literature and art kept pace with a spread of education that embraced Greeks and non-Greeks alike. Although there was a trend in taste towards the sensational, and virtuosity was apt to take the place of refined emotion, the standards of accomplishment remained uniformly high, and technical brilliance made up for many of the deficiencies of creative genius. The demand for copies of the Hellenic masterpieces, meanwhile, never ceased to expand, and occasionally craftsmen produced a work like the Venus de Milo (about 250 B.C.), which breathed all the noble idealism of a former age. Architecture, too, despite a readiness to be impressed by mere size, showed

38

astonishing vigour, and besides adding to the Seven Wonders of the World, applied its principles of design to everything from town-planning to theatre-seats. In science, the theory of physics and mechanics made rapid strides, whilst mathematics set a pace that has only been excelled in our own modern times. Euclid and Archimedes are but two of a long list of names that have come down to us, and that were as famous then as they are now. Likewise, geographers, historians and zoologists made the knowledge of the few the interest of the many, and astronomers unfolded the secrets of the heavens for all to read.

It was a time of enlightenment as well as prosperity, and the thirst for knowledge and entertainment grew rapidly from year to year. Nor did Greek inventiveness lack the means to satisfy it, and a steady tide of fashion flowed through the age.

3

We are now able to perceive in its broadest outline the object of attachment that took the place of the former political interests and supplied the motive force for all this broadening civilization. It was idealism still, but with much more limited aims. The ideal that men set before themselves was no longer the proud hero of liberty whose sphere was everything human and superhuman alike, but the cultured man of the world. Money was the first consideration—not for its own sake, but for what it would bring; and the secret was to make it bring the right things. Art and literature ceased to be the expression of a noble idealism, so losing their idealistic character, and it was rather for the pleasures they brought and the part they played in the make-up of the cultured man that they remained the objects of pursuit. Hence the taste for technique and virtuosity. Hence, too, the movement away from universality. For when men ceased to move on the larger stage of life and were excluded from the things of vital moment, then the major conflicts of will and the deeper emotions of drama failed to have meaning. They were drawn to the domestic, the intimate and the petty. The comedy of manners, not Athenian tragedy, was the type and product of the age.

Thus, in proportion as the goal they set themselves was near and easy of attainment, so was their accomplishment the less, and despite the high general level that was reached, the peaks of achievement exceeded the mediocre at an ever-decreasing rate. As the age proceeded, the powers of creative genius waned for lack of urgent incentive, and it became clear that the idealism of the age was not itself an original and originating thing, but the backwash of an earlier movement that was slowly ebbing away. Morale was gone, and men knew it. For achievement is born of enthusiasm, and their enthusiasms were side-tracked to the trivial and the commonplace. They felt the need of emotional outlet, but could only find the sensational to supply it, and when one sensation was played out, there was only another to supplant it. External life had lost its value.

So it becomes clear that the failure of their idealism was not in its intellectual and æsthetic aspects only; they needed also the fillip of spiritual regeneration. They lacked incentive to make them heighten their ideals and look beyond the actual to a world of better things. It was a moral failing too; and men looked at the brilliance of their cities in vain.

4

We saw in the chapter on Athens that philosophical thought had already begun to turn to the subject of individual character and wrestle with the problem of its improvement, and naturally in an individualist world this side of philosophy received more and more emphasis. It was natural, too, that, whereas in the larger days of Athens, Plato, perceiving the need for moral idealism, had plumped for the highest ideal his boundless imagination could conceive, the philosophers of a later day set a limited objective and sought an opiate instead. Stoicism and Epicureanism, the most popular philosophies of the age, gained a wide acceptance and at times infused a noble intensity of purpose, but they were rather the creeds of resignation than the spurs to action. They recognized and incorporated the new social virtues we have seen, and connected the precepts of morality in some way with a clear conscience, that negative sort of happiness, but they lacked the power to rouse the enthusiastic faith that moves mountains and makes death its only obstacle.

In agony of despair, men and women turned to religion as they had never done before, and even sought for spiritual comfort and reassurance in the mystical faiths of the East. Amongst many others, the Egyptian worship of Isis and Judaism gained thousands of proselytes, but their asceticism, and particularly the circumcision of Judaism, were alien and often horrible to the rational mind of the Greek. Viewed by and large, they made little impression, except insofar as they modified the intellectual aspect of popular philosophy. Religion could and did bring much benefit to individuals, but it was powerless to exert a social influence till the birth of Christianity.

The Hellenistic kingdoms of the Eastern Mediterranean were thus smitten with a mortal disease from the outset. Despite all their glitter of achievement, they were living only in the dying reflection of an earlier age, and the failure of their idealism created a vicious circle from which only fresh forces could save them. Fortunately for the world, such a force was rising in the West, and it was destined to have the power to inspire new strength and give a moral uplift which would make Hellenism live on for many centuries to come. Rome was already, by 200 B.C., mistress of the Western Mediterranean, and all the triumphs of Macedonian arms could avail nothing against her. At the first impact with the West, which came within a decade, the rottenness of Hellenistic autocracy was revealed, and in spite of her great reluctance to advance, Rome was compelled to take over kingdom after kingdom, until eventually they were all incorporated as provinces of the Roman Empire. As we shall see later, Rome, with all her failings, was a power for good, and Hellenistic civilization merged into Græco-Roman to gain sustenance and a new vigour that would carry it over the whole known world.

CHAPTER V

THE RISE OF NATIONALIST EUROPE

I

WE HAVE just seen how Macedonian arms were instrumental in carrying the culture of the Greece they conquered to vast new territories which readily adopted the flourishing civilization; we shall now see the same story repeated in modern Europe. For the mixture of old and new political entities, France, Spain and Germany, who had been lured into Italy by the wealth and brilliance of her new society and had ended by smashing it with their depredations, took back with them the new learning and culture they had found and spread them abroad as effectively as had been done in the earlier age. From then on, the Renaissance grew progressively till it embraced not only the three original marauders, but the whole of the continent of Europe. Already by 1530, when Benvenuto Cellini, the sculptor and jeweller, visited Paris, he was meeting strong competition from the beginning of things in France. A century later there was the Dutch Renaissance culminating in the paintings of Rembrandt, and another hundred years later still Peter the Great was building his new capital at St. Petersburg to signalize the rebirth of Russia.

Moreover, in 1492 there had occurred an event which shifted the whole balance of history. Columbus discovered America, and this, together with the discovery of the Cape route to India a few years earlier, opened up new vistas of conquest and wealth, which not only intensified the movement in Western Europe, but also carried it to colonies in completely new lands.

Wherever it spread, the effects were no less remarkable than in Italy. Feudalism was broken down, and new political units, the nationalist states of modern Europe, stood firmer on the ruins. They were all monarchies, with the reins of government securely in the hands of their kings, and the royal Courts put on a magnificence that was as costly as it was imposing. The dynastic game of territorial expansion began afresh, but there was a corresponding fillip to labour and commerce that enabled economic prosperity to keep pace with the growing expenditure. The introduction of gunpowder, too, had given the European an indisputable superiority over the peoples of other continents, and he was able to force his way into new territories, which the recent discoveries had opened to him, and these served to subsidize his development.

Each of the nations produced its own variant expression of the arts, which, though manifestly of the parent stock, yet received fresh vigour from the new national setting. In literature this was especially so; and the fact that Shakespeare stands so far above Renaissance writers of other nations is merely the measure of Shakespeare's stature. Architecture was slower off the mark, but quickly made up for lost time, and ended by transforming the world's appearance as effectively as Copernicus had transformed its astronomy. The youngest child of the arts, the new music of Italy, found particular favour on all sides, and by the genius of Purcell, Bach and Handel grew to achieve "undreamt of miracles of sound". In the realm of thought the story was the same. The fetters of mediæval authority were shaken off, and men launched themselves on the sea of speculation. Bacon and Descartes sounded the return to scientific principles, and began that reign of inductive reasoning that was to be so increasingly prolific of results.

It was a time of stirring and upheaval unprecedented in extent, and when everything changed, the difficulty is to sort out the most salient features of the change. Once again, therefore, we will use our survey of the ancient world to point the way, and attempt a comparison with the Hellenistic Age of Greece.

2

The first thing that emerges from the process of comparison, however, is an important difference. Whereas the literary achievement, for example, of the Hellenistic Age in no case equalled the best of the Hellenic, the literature of the Renaissance in Spain, France and England often equalled, and sometimes surpassed, that of its counterpart in Italy. We must seek to account for a difference of this sort, therefore, before we can admit the comparableness of the two periods.

It has already been indicated that the literature of the time gained considerably from its new national setting, and we shall find that it was the demand of the new nationalistic spirit for expression that was responsible for the splendid heights to which the literature rose. For nationalism was not only a product of the age, but was itself a motivating force of immense power, and made each of the new states it erected bear some resemblance to a larger Athens or a regional Florence. We must therefore consider briefly the nature of this new factor and assess its importance in the whole.

The creation of these new nations, France, Spain, England, etc., was governed mainly by two factors—the demand for centralization of authority, and the geo- and ethnographic circumstances conditioning that demand. The old feudal organization had cut right through mere matters of geography and race, as for example in the Norman kingdom, which had comprised not only England but a large part of France as well, and, more glaringly still, in the Holy Roman Empire, which bore no relationship to anything whatsoever; and the results, politically and socially, had been chaotic. Neither efficient nor strong government had been possible, and local barons had been able to make hay of such organization as there was, with no one to say them nay. The crying need everywhere was for an effective central authority, which would suppress the war-lords and give as large an area as possible the peace and security that progress required. A large single

43

unit had proved a failure; small units the size of shires or duchies would be no improvement. In the event, language and geography in most cases set a natural frontier for which the communications of the time were adequate, and within these bounds the existing kings set themselves to establish a uniform government. The support given to the kings by the rising commercial interests was often instrumental in cementing the new national unity, and the part played by capitals such as London and Paris often gave them a unique position in their countries.

Only in Germany and the Low Countries was the new movement frustrated. For the incubus of the Holy Roman Empire proved fatal to natural development; and then, when the Lutheran Reformation split the allegiance of the whole race into two opposing camps, the mania that afflicted them completed their dismemberment by flinging them into the horrors of the Thirty Years' War. In Austria and elsewhere the Hapsburgs gathered up the broken fragments of the Empire with grasping fingers, and settled down at Vienna to repair their fortunes by marriage, alliance and treachery.

We thus have a picture of monarchist States springing up all over Europe, just as we saw in the Eastern Mediterranean after Alexander's conquests—but with this difference, that the various States each have their own language and customs which it is their pride to defend and improve. Despite the universal Latinity of the age, it is in French, Spanish and English that the new masterpieces of literature are written, just as it was in Italian that Ariosto and Tasso wrote theirs. To the mighty incentive of the Italian Renaissance, therefore, is added the glowing ardour of local patriotism. It is not just the spreading and development of one culture, as in the Hellenistic Age, but the founding of as many new cultures as there are nations. The French, the Spanish, the Dutch or the Russian Renaissances are all separate edifices, each built on the twin foundations of native propensity and foreign precept. For this reason there are differences in time, taste and accomplishment, and for this reason, too, the effects were deeper and more glorious.

Nevertheless, this clarification of the differences enables us to see the points of contact between them all the more clearly. The first stirrings in each case arose from the example given in Italy, and the added impulse they received in their own countries was always of the same sort—that of nationalism. Judged from the standpoint of European civilization as a whole, therefore, the Renaissance may be considered as a single movement, started by the re-discovery of Greek culture in Italy, and passing over Europe as a wave that gathers renewed strength with every frontier crossed. The point at which it differs from the spread of Hellenism lies in the increased impetus that it received from a nation-wide patriotism as it burst on each country in turn, and in considering it as one movement, therefore, we must inspect its general trend, not so much in the moment of its initial enthusiasm, but after it had settled down to an established order of things over the continent as a whole. Provided we keep an eye to such permanent results as accrued from the new nationalism, a comparison with the Hellenistic Age will then be permissible.

3

The salient tendencies we found in the Hellenistic Age were a broadening of society and a simultaneous failure of idealism, and in the mainstream of the Renaissance in continental Europe the same features may be seen again. The movement began with all the enthusiasm that a return to humanism and patriotism could give it, and it achieved the triumphs of art, literature and social brilliance we have already observed. Then gradually we see it lose momentum, droop and finally sink into a stagnant society that would need fresh impulse to make it continue progress.

At first the breakdown of Feudalism which the erection of nationalist States had completed gave men the same opportunity for self-expression that had been seized so readily in the cities of Italy, and the model of Italian culture, often backed by their own reading of the Greek prototypes, crystallized their vague aspirations into conscious and subconscious ideals that directed their development. The joy of self-expression, too, was enhanced by the patriotic fervour that the new national status inspired, and for a time there was that same balance of individual and communal effort that we have found before in the peak of Athenian achievement. That the men of the Renaissance were individualists is true; that they were at the same time patriots is also true; and the very eagerness to excel which personal liberty aroused, was proudly directed to the benefit of the nation that permitted them this freedom. Men laboured for the ideal of national independence, and they sought to glorify the figure of their king as the personification of their every effort.

The men who took part in this resurgence were newcomers. They were the followers of the Crown who had helped to subdue the barons who were impeding unity—small landowners, merchants, soldiers and sailors—and their occupations gained both in value and prestige with the new way of life. Society broadened to include them and took on, with their entry, a larger and more cultured aspect. The arts began to have place and respect, and the contacts of commerce widened their outlook.

They were also the new executive of the monarchical government, gaining thereby official status as well. But they were still the servants of the Crown, and the Crown was all-powerful. Freedom did not extend into the political sphere, and opposition to the royal policy was inevitably treason. Where grievances or personal inclination led to disagreement with the king, silence or a *coup d'état* was the only alternative; and without remission of the royal prerogatives, therefore, the stage was already set in advance for a separation of national and private interests, as in the Hellenistic kingdoms. With the growth of economic prosperity on the Continent this tendency was actually set in motion. Merchants pursued their own commercial interests independently of the State, and a large official class arose whose only concern was the holding of royal incumbencies. In these circumstances the loosening of national ties was not long in making itself felt, and by the end of the 17th century the traditional leaders of Europe—France, Spain and Austria— were all fast stagnating into the ponderous, reactionary despotisms that Macedon, Syria and Egypt had been before them.

There was another factor that contributed to the decline. Except in the north of Europe the Reformation had been stamped out, and the Catholic Counter-Reformation had imposed the millstone of mediæval theology on the fresh vigour of the Renaissance. The demand for reform in the Church had originally been a healthy sign of moral and religious growth, coming not only from enlightened laymen, but also from devoted servants of the Church itself, and schism had been the last intention of the Reformers. But the bigotry of Papal advocates, combined with the blundering obstinacy of militant Germans, had precipitated the worst sort of dilemma in which extremism ran riot. The Catholic Church went in one direction—backwards; Protestantism went in a thousand others. The Church, on its part, tied itself to a system of antiquated logic which was diametrically opposed to the new experimental outlook of the Renaissance, and as the governments of Spain, France and Austria, the major Powers of Europe, were staunchly Catholic, the resources of the State were added to the terrors of the Inquisition to burn out the hiding-places of free and original thinking. Scientific progress was thus checked, and freedom of expression received a setback which did irreparable damage to society.

By the 18th century the continent of Europe showed the results of these tendencies all too clearly. The monarchies of Spain, France and Austria were not only moribund, but they had set their faces firmly against any remedial measures. The broadening of society had come to a full stop; continual war had raised expenditure to a level at which it was crippling commerce; and a lack of incentive was draining the life even out of agriculture. Serious as these matters were in themselves, they were aggravated by a rapid rise in the population. The prosperity of the 17th century had given an impetus to the birth-rate which was carrying it well out of reach of the economic possibilities of the time, and as outlets were barred by the strict social order, unemployment and poverty were assuming ominous proportions. Nor were things better in art and literature. A classical preciseness that followed the first enthusiastic fullness of the Renaissance had given place to a jejune artificiality that smacked of staleness and failing inspiration, and technical novelty, sensationalism and senti-mentality were the recourse of imaginative deficiency. Even in decoration the splendid correctness of Versailles degenerated into the pallid eclecticism of Louis Seize. The wheel was come full circle. It was the 2nd century B.C. all over again.

4

After what we have seen elsewhere, the idealism that was responsible for the original impetus of the European Renais-sance will now be quite clear, as also will the reasons for its subsequent failure. The opportunity for self-expression that came with the new society was at first limited by the spirit of co-operation on which that society depended, and men spent themselves on the ideal of national independence which they personified in the figure of their king. Such a society prospered, as it was bound to. Then came the separa-tion of political and private interests, which was fatal to corporate effort on a national scale, and individualism de-graded their ideals correspondingly. Patriotism tended to become the monopoly of a single class to whom it meant autocracy and aggression, and co-operation did not reach

47

beyond the members of the same stratum of society. At the same time, authoritarianism clamped down on the free development of thought, so that creative endeavour was robbed of its incentive and the enlightenment of authority failed to keep pace with the growing problems of the age. Spain and Austria dropped right out of the world of intellect, and French *élan* was directed mainly to the satisfaction of royal vainglory. Art and literature suffered the same deterioration, and manifestly in the 18th century men were living in the dying reflection of a previous achievement. They had the mode of an earlier age, but none of its inspiration.

Yet this was not all. Though their ideals were lowered from the plane of liberty and independence, they lost their ambition to raise them. The "Grande Monarchie" of Louis XIV was both the peak and goal of continental achievement, and henceforward there was nothing but feebler imitation. Versailles was the culmination of Medicean magnificence, and kings and princes were blinded by it. Ambition was satisfied. The moral failing that we found in the Hellenistic Age was thus prevalent also in the monarchies of 18th-century Europe, and moral idealism had gone the way of intellectual and æsthetic.

Just as in the earlier epoch, a similar inadequacy of the external world had turned men's thoughts inward for spiritual comfort, so was the trend again, but so again was it barren. The claims of the individual conscience that the Reformation had raised had been ruthlessly put down, and Roman Catholicism offered only the remedy of amputation. At the price of unconditional surrender, the Mother Church would give welcome to the fold, but made no provision for the social and mental development of her flock. Moreover, the attempt of intellectuals to reconcile the conflicting theories of science and theology had led merely to the creed of Deism, which provided neither comfort nor inspiration. For an intellectual idea of a transcendental God such as the 18th-century Deists erected was less than useless for the needs of the ordinary man; it even compared unfavourably with the Platonism that the 17th century had re-discovered. Morality and religion thus ceased to be mutually propellant, and while self-interest and sentimentalism replaced them on the one side, nihilism and anarchy were preparing on the other.

An *impasse* had been reached from which the resources of the continental monarchies were powerless to extricate them, and their civilization was faced with inevitable collapse unless fresh forces could be found to revive it. Already by the middle of the 18th century the rumble of enormous masses of submerged humanity could be heard, heaving with discontent, and an explosion was imminent. In France, where the population had risen the fastest, the danger was at its most critical, but signs were not lacking in Spain, Austria and elsewhere that all was far from well. Yet the Governments had neither the will nor the means to allay them. Their traditional policy of suppression had so effectively dulled their senses and sensibilities that they could not see either why or how they should bring about the changes that the situation demanded, and Louis XV could only cynically exclaim, "Aprés moi le déluge". Human fertility and human inertia had created a situation from which only human ingenuity could save them; yet the rulers of Europe were sunk in an apathy that was almost oriental in its completeness.

England alone remained active, and it was England that provided both the physical and spiritual means of escape. English Industrialism and English Liberalism were the two great forces that were to inspire a new beginning and save the old. France, it is true, was blown sky high for the moment in the Jacobin Revolution, and Spain and Austria lingered on to die a natural death in the 20th century. But European civilization had been saved, and a whole world would be leavened by it.

5

We have now reached the point at which two great civilizations have degenerated through internal failure and must face collapse without the infusion of new vigour from outside. As has been said, this revivifying effect is indeed supplied by the peoples of Rome and England respectively, and it is to them that we must now turn for an indication of the kind of forces which they set in motion. They had both been contemporaries of the earlier movements we have inspected, but their development had been slower and more individual, and, for that reason, more certain. We will therefore review briefly their histories up to the same point of time that we have reached with Greek and European civilizations as a whole, so as to discover their special characteristics. We can then discover more particularly the nature of the contributions they made at the two crises of the general evolution.

CHAPTER VI

ROME

I

THE FOUNDING of the city of Rome is one of those events that have become too dimmed by the passage of time for us to distinguish them clearly, but it is assigned by tradition to the year 753 B.C. The town was apparently an outpost erected on the low hills overlooking the first fordable crossing of the Tiber. It was intended for the protection of Latium, the district just south of the river, against the Etruscans who lived to the north of it, and was thus from the start populated by a hardy, pioneering element drawn from the people of Latium as a whole. Nevertheless, at first it failed signally in its ostensible duty, as it was captured by the enemy, and remained in their hands till the end of the 6th century B.C.—a fate doubtless deplored at the time, but of inestimable value to posterity.

The Latins were an Aryan people, part of the huge migration which had entered Italy at about the same time as it swamped the Balkans, but the Etruscans are even more wrapped in obscurity than early Rome itself. Fancy has made many flights of conjecture about their origin, but it seems most likely that they came to Italy from Asia Minor or the Levant. The important thing is that they were a completely different race from the Latins, and gave the stalwarts of Rome an admixture of blood which not only differentiated them from their neighbours, but strengthened and vitalized them beyond the ordinary.

After the eventual expulsion of the Tarquins, their Etruscan overlords, the situation that faced the Romans was similar to that of the Athenians in or about the same year, 510 B.C. Their experiences had given them a hatred of despotism which permeated their history for five centuries, and they were determined on freedom and independence. They therefore required a constitution which would embody a proper respect for the rights of the individual and give them the liberty of action they desired for themselves; but the way in which they solved their problem distinguishes them radically from their Athenian contemporaries. Democracy was undoubtedly in the air at this time, and democratic principles were laid down from the start, but the Romans were too conservative, too practical, to go the "whole hog" straight away. They allowed themselves to be convinced of the necessity for authority and discipline, and were willing that the experience and greater sense of responsibility of the aristocrats should direct their republic, at least at the outset. Instead therefore of extreme democracy being set up within half a century, as at Athens, it was over two hundred years before the original goal of equal voting-power and equal opportunity for office was finally reached, and then with certain modifications that we shall see.

In the meantime, the patriotism that the mere idea of the commonwealth inspired, and the confidence that they placed in the aristocratic government, more than justified themselves. By 270 B.C. Rome had risen by easy stages to be mistress of the whole of Italy from the Po southwards, and had also beaten off a serious threat from Greece in the shape of a would-be imitator of Alexander the Great. Moreover, by apparent chance, the Romans had hit on a system of government which put the whole of Italy behind them and made Italians willing, as well as bound, to accept Roman hegemony. This was the same system of gradual enfranchisement that had been applied with such signal success in Rome itself and brought participation in the full rights and privileges of Romans to be the goal of non-Romans as well. It was a policy as novel as it was enlightened, and made Rome come not as a destroyer, but as a guide to better things. For Roman citizenship by this time had not only political rights to offer, but commercial and social advantages also. Already every road in Italy led to Rome, and she had become the hub of Italian life. The Greek colonial cities of the south coast still did a flourishing trade with the Eastern Mediterranean, but Rome was the entrepôt through which their wares reached the interior, and Roman strategy had their fleets and resources at its disposal.

Hard days still lay ahead, however, and with the year 264 B.C. Rome was impelled into a series of Great Wars which lasted more than a century and conclusively changed the course of her development. First, between 264 B.C. and 202 B.C., with an interval of only twenty-eight years, she was engaged in a life-and-death struggle with Carthage. This was a city near the site of the modern Tunis, which controlled a vast mercantile empire in the Western Mediterranean and on the Atlantic seaboard, and Romans fought in Sicily,

Spain and Africa, as well as repulsing an all-but-successful invasion of Italy itself, which lasted twelve years and dealt Italian productivity a blow from which it never completely recovered. Only the superior stamina of Rome and her more far-sighted policy eventually won the war, and the collapse of Carthage in 202 B.C. left her the exhausted but undisputed mistress of everything west of the Straits of Sicily.

Of breathing-space, however, there was to be none, for almost at once she was embroiled in the Balkans. The Hellenistic kingdom of Macedon had viewed with disquiet the rise of a new power across the Adriatic and had given a certain amount of ineffectual aid to Carthage at the height of the struggle. Rome did not forget this attempted stab in the back, and now that the menace was over, was in a mood to be truculent. Diplomatic exchanges soon gave place to open war and, the Macedonian phalanx proving no match for the Roman legion, Rome emerged completely victorious in 188 B.C. For the moment, direct government was not imposed, but after various experiments in partial autonomy had led merely to serious rebellion, first Macedon in 169 B.C. and then Greece proper in 146 B.C. were taken over into the general provincial administration.

2

As has been indicated, this long story of war and conquest was not without important repercussions on the government and politics of Rome. The waging of war demands a single-ness of aim and a concentration of authority that accord in no way with democracy, and a century of war requires a con-tinuity of policy beyond the scope of a single democratic leader. To this problem Rome found the answer indeed within her own democratic institutions, but in doing so lost her democracy. Like everything Roman, this was not a single or a deliberate step, but just came about gradually with the years.

Under the completed democracy of 287 B.C. the people in conclave were supreme. They elected the executive officials annually and superintended all legislation. They decided policy, both internal and external, and any one of them could himself assume the highest office of State on election. But there also existed a second chamber, the Senate, which had been the controlling body during the novitiate of the democracy and which still survived in a purely advisory capacity. Its prestige and seniority enabled it to exert a strong influence on the counsels of the republic, and it was this body which acted as the presiding genius of Rome during the long period of wars. It was comprised solely of men who had held official positions in the State, both military and civil, and represented the nearest thing to a "Brains Trust" the ancient world ever possessed. Moreover, it was permanent and wieldy, being maintained at about 600 life-members, and could give the continuity and centralization of authority that the times demanded. In the long absence at the front of the able-bodied men who constituted both electorate and parliament, it became the *de facto* government of Rome, and the "advice" of the Senate came automatically to assume the force of law. Democracy survived only in theory.

There was also another important factor at work which further closed the governmental monopoly of the Senate, and that was the Roman belief in inherited ability. If a man proved his worth as a general or a statesman, it was held that his descendants must be equally worthy, and the Romans continued to elect them to office, and so to the Senate, for generation after generation. There could have been no more effectual way of building up an hereditary official class in their midst, and indeed by the end of the war with Carthage, the Senate was recruited almost exclusively from a limited number of families. These alone had the confidence of the electorate, and soon began to look upon official position and Senatorial rank as a natural adjunct of birth. They constituted an emergent nobility controlling the Roman Republic through its special council, the Senate; and the people merely supplied perfunctory ratification of its proceedings.

In these circumstances the Senate's greatness was shown not only in the triumphant direction it gave to Roman foreign policy and military effort, but also in its maintenance of the "home front" and public morale. Finance and psychology were its strong points no less than grand strategy, and national enthusiasm for the "commonwealth" never once wavered through all the gruelling years of war. The nobility had a tradition of service to the State which permeated public life, and their integrity did not come in question. Senate and people were at one: together they formed an invincible combination.

3

This outline, brief as it is, is sufficient to indicate what were the main features of Roman character. They were an intensely conscientious and hard-working people, dogged enough to be obstinate, and practical to the point of genius. Their achievements were not the illumination of a moment, but the hard-won reward of experience, and they changed their pre-conceived ideas only so far as was necessary to make them practicable. They were thoroughly unimaginative and illiterate, and their history of continual warfare successfully prevented their becoming otherwise. They had neither art nor literature, science nor wit; but they had a language that for brevity, point and grandeur was unsurpassable. It was a language to be used, not to be played with, and seemed designed specifically for government and law. Law, indeed, was the fundamental of Roman mentality—both for its diligent protection of individual rights and for its limitation of them for the common good. The Roman spirit of independence was magnificent: their sense of discipline was overwhelming.

The Romans themselves attributed their success to three qualities—a due sense of responsibility (*gravitas*), self-respect (*dignitas*) and awe of authority, whether religious, State or paternal (*pietas*)—and these were indeed the outward signs of that tremendous power which the Romans manifested in all their actions. Because they had a deep sense of their responsibilities, they were conscientious; because they prided themselves on their personal qualities, they were obstinate; and because they respected authority, they were disciplined and patriotic. But that these qualities existed, and continued to exist, was due to a deeper psychological reason. They were unwitting idealists. The Romans' ideals were not of the intellect or the æsthetic sensibilities, but they felt them with the whole of their moral being. They had an ideal of unflinching service to family and State that guided them throughout and filled them with an over-riding sense of duty. Their actual morals were no better than those of their time; but their feeling for the obligations of such morality as they understood wholly distinguished them from their contemporaries.

Only less decisive was their talent for the practical. If their moral idealism made them masters of themselves, their practicality made them masters of the world. In the sphere of action they could turn their hands to anything, and by dint of perseverance eventually did it better than the others. Where no precedent existed, then they hammered one out from their own traditions, and, as it were without noticing, became originators on a vast scale. For this reason, too, they were thorough, and whatever they did was done to last. Whether

54

we turn to their roads, their walls, their language, their system of law or their principles of administration, we find the same quality of practical thoroughness which has made them objects of admiration for all time. Enduring themselves, they built a world to outlast them.

4

This, then, was the character of the people who found themselves face to face with the degenerate civilization of the Hellenistic kingdoms, and will they, nill they, saddled with its maintenance and resuscitation. In everything they were diametrically opposed to the Greeks they had to rule. They had achieved none of the triumphs of art, literature and science so essential to Greek culture, and the word "theory" was alien to their minds. Yet they had wrought out of their primitive traditions what all the brilliance of Greek intellect had failed most lamentably to produce—a workable system of human government—and though starting at the same time as the Greeks, were not yet at the zenith of their power, when Greece was long past her best.

Faced with a situation that imperilled their whole life and livelihood in the Punic Wars, they had not allowed attachment to their personal rights to stand in the way of the common weal, but had accepted a narrowing of the governmental basis in the interests of efficiency and discipline. They had relaxed none of their corporate ardour and had surmounted all their obstacles. Both Government and people shared in this identification of interests, and the Senate set an example of conscientious devotion to duty that was an inspiration to the humblest legionary. A moral strength in which the Greeks were so signally lacking was the secret of their power, and this was combined with a practical ability that Greek theorizing seldom or never envisaged.

The impact of two such opposite outlooks was bound to be fraught with the utmost significance, but before we go on to consider the effects on both Romans and Greeks, and the nature of the civilization that emerged from their association, we will first review similarly the history of England, and attempt to elucidate the special characteristics of its people which enabled them to influence civilization no less remarkably than the Romans.

CHAPTER VII

ENGLAND

I

IN ACCORDANCE with our purposes, this chapter will not attempt to give a concise history of England, but will merely draw attention to those features of it which principally differentiated her development from that of her European contemporaries, and which constitute the chain of causes leading up to her significant entry into world affairs. We may note for a start, then, that England has always partaken of the racial characteristics of two great branches of European peoples—the Germanic and the Latin—and in her early history she leaned first one way and then the other, never finally committing herself, until at last the moment came when she could stand on her own feet. She was then able to strike out a special development of her own, with something of the features of both. Her population and her culture alike were drawn from the two sources, though at different times and in differing extent, and for centuries England was a melting-pot to which North and South alike contributed. It may be noted, too, that in all the successive invasions of Anglo-Saxons, Vikings and Normans, it was the hardiest and most adventurous types that formed the bulk of the settlers; so that England's primary population was thus a mixture of the best of northern Europe's peoples.

Everything conspired to detach them from Europe. The Norman Conquest finally put an end to Canute's dream of a vast Danish empire centred on England, and broke her close connection with the Scandinavian countries for ever; but just as conclusively the rise of nationalism in France put an end to Plantagenet visions of a continental career and threw England back upon herself. The anarchy of the Wars of the Roses ensued. Then, within seven years of each other, two major events occurred which gave a new direction to English history. In 1485 Henry Tudor won his way to the throne at Bosworth Field, and in 1492 Columbus discovered America. The Tudors, riding on the crest of the wave of nationalism that we have seen, welded England into a nation and gave her back the unity and spirit that had produced Agincourt, Crécy and Chaucer. But the discovery of America provided this spirit with a fresh field of action, so that if the continent of Europe was closed, adventure could be sought instead on the Spanish Main and the road to Eldorado. It did more. From being a remote appendage to a continent, the British Isles became the new centre of gravity of a larger world, able to turn wheresoever opportunity offered, and dominating the new highways of ships and commerce. England began to put her immense energy into exploiting this new position, and within little more than a century had cut herself off almost completely from European entanglements.

Two further factors made for isolation. England had adopted the Reformation, originally from royal expediency, but later from conviction, and though for the moment she seemed in danger of being embroiled in the German chaos, the operation of a second factor speedily led to her withdrawal. This was an internal dilemma arising from the Stuart attempt to erect a monarchy on the continental model, but which accorded in no way with the spirited English views on liberty and independence. As a consequence, almost the whole of the 17th century was spent in working out an acceptable form of government, and the resultant Parliamentary system served to carry her farther away than ever from the sympathies of France, Spain and Austria.

The cultural connection with the Continent was equally loose and spasmodic. We have already seen that the Renaissance tended to go its own way when once within the various national boundaries, and England was no exception. In literature, indeed, her native romanticism found a particularly fertile field, and Shakespeare and Milton carried her achievements to a plane no other nation could approach. Elizabethan architecture, too, was her own accomplishment, and Byrd gave standing to her natural utterance of song. Later, the effects of French classicism were strongly felt, and even an academy was mooted after the French example, but the dominating influence of Dryden was thrown heavily into the balance on the side of native tradition, and a deep obligation did not turn to subservience.

By the end of the 17th century England had not only withdrawn from the mainstream of European development, but she seemed to have sacrificed her finest chances through internal dissidence. Yet with the turn of the century her period of withdrawal was proved to be one, not of decline, but of consolidation, and the genius of Marlborough burst upon a startled world and established England in the forefront of European nations. Her main interest still lay outside the Continent, however, and her interference in continental affairs was not permanent, being confined to dominance of the Low Countries for her own security. The North American colonies, India and the routes to this overseas empire were the things she cared for most, because of the scope they gave to her mounting volume of trade. Thus when George III came to the throne in 1760 England had risen on the back of continental decadence to be the premier maritime, commercial and colonial Power of the world, holding in fee both the gorgeous East and the golden West.

2

From this brief outline the independent attitude of England as a nation is clearly visible; and the attitude of individual Englishmen throughout this time was one of no less sterling independence. From the earliest times the people had shown a disposition to stand up for their liberties, and even in the feudal era the "villeins", and particularly the "burghers" of England had never allowed themselves to sink to the same level of degradation as their counterparts on the Continent. It was partly for this reason that the Renaissance flourished there so vigorously, as the opportunity for self-expression came to men with the initiative to use it to the full. Nevertheless, they also had a strong tradition of co-operation, and Tudor nationalism only intensified a patriotism that had existed long before. Their island position had already given them a feeling for racial homogeneity, when boundaries hardly signified elsewhere, and the suppression of the barons removed the last obstacle to a whole-hearted unity of purpose. In all the divided counsel that followed, the motive was never in doubt, and difference of opinion, though it brought the country low, had always its welfare at heart.

There were two great issues that arose to trouble the land— one of religion, and the other of the constitution. Men demanded the right to live and worship as they liked, and for more than a century they gave life and limb for their principles. Yet all who fought, all who protested their freedom to the death, objected strenuously to the implication that this right ever brought their patriotism into question: if they were High Church and royalist, they felt their affections were self-evident; if they were Puritan and parliamentary, they were no less determined to preserve their hard-won liberties for
58

England. Laud and Milton alike were unshakeable patriots. Hence it was that the problems were resolved, not by the final supremacy of one party or the other, but by a compromise that gave them both the right to live and work in their own way for the common good. The theory was abandoned for the substance, and though the systems of religious and political government that emerged were neither systematic nor clearly defined, they had the precious quality of being workable, and, furthermore, lent themselves to progressive modification. They were practical, unpretentious, living things that grew because they gradually admitted everyone who applied, and worked because they stressed the spirit, not the letter.

The Revolution Settlement of 1689 was the corner-stone of English liberty, and out of it arose the triple-working harmony of Crown, Lords and Commons, which was unique in contemporary Europe. It was not democracy, but neither was it an aristocratic despotism. According to their lights, the ruling-class played fair and managed the country in its best interests and with a minimum of interference with personal freedom. They had a tradition of service, born of long struggle for independence, and gave the best scope they understood to personal prejudice and ability. Moreover, it was a tradition of honour, and though commerce raced ahead, its interests never separated from the Government's, because merchants played their part in politics with landowners and took their share of responsibility as well as of success. Despite the corruption of the early 18th century, the Parliaments of the day gave value for their money, and the strength that was gathering in the diligent pursuit of colonies and commerce came brilliantly to light beneath the wizard's touch of Chatham.

3

We can now see the secret of Englishmen's success. Unlike subjects of the continental monarchies, they remained free men in full control of their destinies; and unlike the central Europeans, they overcame their internal incompatibilities. They thus had opportunity and incentive both for individual and corporate effort, and could apply themselves equally to both without hindrance or stint. They might differ, and did; they could be bigoted, and were so; but they learned to be tolerant in the last resort, and they abided by the ultimate decisions of their fellow-countrymen. The spirit of compromise tempered their individualism, and an understanding of the obligations of society took the roughness from their strong attachment to principle.

Nor are the reasons for this far to seek. For they were idealists—not consciously or aggressively so, but nevertheless intensely; and the force of idealism was a motive throughout their history. Hence came the spur to action, and hence the guiding hand to their boundless energy, so that they had the will-power to endeavour, and their effort had a communal aim. But that is not all. It is important to observe that the English ideal developed with themselves, and always stayed ahead of their attainment, so that ambition was never satisfied and incentive was permanently with them. Thus they did not become decadent or ever cease to progress, but continued their development when the rest of Europe was fast sinking into the 18th-century decline. So important to our theme is this feature of English character that we must stop a moment to consider its working and take a simple example of the process in operation in order to perceive its significance.

Edmund Spenser's allegorical poem, "The Faerie Queene", was written during the last two decades of the 16th century, as the literary Renaissance of England came near to its full flowering. It was a time when the new Tudor society was just finding its feet, having conclusively supplanted the old baronial aristocracy, and men were filled with a restlessness that might lead them anywhere. The old ideals were gone, outmoded, and the ethics of society were in a period of interregnum. In this situation, Spenser set himself to erect imaginatively a new ideal that would serve his generation of Englishmen and supply them with both an aim and an incentive for a fuller life. A vague feeling of patriotism that was manifesting itself in the glorification of Elizabeth was to be seized and moulded to the purpose of concentrating endeavour. In the English manner, he reverenced tradition, and only beheld the triumphs of the future through the accomplishments of the past. Nothing would be stable but what had its foundations deeply laid in the bedrock of time, and the present could live only if firmly rooted in the past. A society that had just emerged with the Tudor settlement, therefore, and which had no immediate connection with the mainstream of English cultural development, must be given one, and made to link itself securely to that society it had replaced.

Now, the previous feudal society at its best had been motivated by the ideal of knighthood, a romantic sense of chivalry whose conceptual basis was service. The Knights of the Round Table are an example of its highest attainment, as the Knight of Chaucer's "Canterbury Tales" is of its homeliest. In practice, they had usually fallen far short of perfection, particularly in the later Middle Ages, and the brutal lords of the York and Lancaster wars had become the type of degenerate knight-errantry. But the ideal had nevertheless been of immense importance in its day, and Spenser saw that it was too valuable to be lost entirely. He therefore decided to recondition it—to bring it up to date and fit it for the new circumstances of life. Every hero that he portrayed in "The Faerie Queene" is ostensibly the legendary knight of English saga, clad in all the accoutrements of feudalism and performing all the doughty deeds of chivalry, and seems at first sight to have stepped straight out of an earlier age. Yet a feeling soon comes over the reader that there is something different about them, that they are anything but the mediæval "toughs" that had been so superficially romanticized in the previous era. They have a new civility and civilian consciousness that are symbolic of a more civilized outlook and differentiate them wholly from Germanic robber-barons. They are, indeed, the Tudor heroes themselves, dressed in the panoply of romance and coloured with the ideals of chivalry. The mystic conception of dedication and service has been imposed on the new feeling for culture and humaneness that emerged with the Renaissance, and a new ideal person is constructed that harmonizes the best of old and new alike. It is an ideal as readily comprehensible as it was inspiring, and by its effect of fitting Elizabethan society into the pattern of English development, helped to concentrate their efforts to a nobler purpose. It gave tangible expression to the lives the best of them lived, and brought into focus their vaguest aspirations. Sir Philip Sydney, for example, was a knight not only of the flaming sword, but of the peaceful arts as well, and it was this gradual transformation of tradition that made him honoured in a nation's eyes: the poet's eye merely extracted its ideological significance and pointed the way clearly to the path of emulation.

It was this spirit that actuated the English throughout. They still looked back to the "good old days" when they also looked forward to the new, and the strength of conservatism was combined with the vigour of enterprise. As their society broadened with the years, the newcomers brought with them their own virtues and fresh interests, but they did not strike out an entirely new line for themselves, as the Italians had

61

done. Instead they attached themselves to the old, and by their contributions leavened and enriched it. In the worst of them it was snobbery; in the best it was innate nobility; and the result was a continuous tradition that overcame the rankest individualist. The ideal to which they sought to assimilate themselves was that of a "gentleman", but the virtues which attached to the quality of "gentlemanliness" were in perpetual evolution, from the "very parfit gentil" man of Chaucer's Knight onwards to the present day.

4

We are now justified in asserting that the idealism of the English was partly of a moral nature, and we may attribute its peculiar efficacy to the fact that it was working in a race with a practical bent. For the English were intensely practical. We have already seen how they excelled in all the arts of peace and war, and evolved a way of life that owed nothing to theory and everything to commonsense; but that is not the whole picture. In morality, too, they gave importance to the lessons of experience, and did not allow their abstractions to lose touch with the facts they represented. Their Christianity, for example, followed the tradition of St. Augustine, laying more stress on the value of holy life than on logical consistency in theology, and though as Protestants they respected the claims of the individual conscience, and as Puritans upheld them, they recognized as a nation that the conscience has its inevitable limitations of habit and environment, and sought the authority of high example as a guide to conduct. This they found in their ubiquitous bibles and persistent ideals, and to live in conformity with their standard was a more powerful urge than all the intellectual persuasions of abstract theology.

Without being particularly moral, they were always moralists—so much so that the besetting fault of their literature was an ever-present tendency to didacticism. They demanded a high standard of integrity in others which necessarily reacted on their own, but laid them open to a charge of hypocrisy from the super-intelligent. It is also true that though in general they showed a solid healthiness of outlook, a Puritan iconoclasm was always close to the surface. Nevertheless, their very lack of logical consistency and their bent for the practical answer prevented them going to extremes, and allowed their preaching and teaching to move with the times. Their morality displayed a parable-like adaptability to growing knowledge, so that their moral ideals stayed ahead of their intellectual attainment, and as new problems confronted them with each age, an ideal solution always presented itself which gave their practical endeavours a direction and an inspiration, and enabled them to win through, however tardily.

Thus, when we compare the characters of Englishmen and Romans, we find that, despite the cultural superiority of the English, the basic factors that made them strong and successful were the same. They were both practical peoples, inspired by a moral idealism which enabled them to help their fellows whilst helping themselves, and kept them united in ultimate purpose through all the tribulations of social and political evolution. With this understanding, we are fortified for a consideration of the actual contributions they made to the progress of their respective civilizations, and this will be the subject of the next two chapters.

CHAPTER VIII

ROMAN CITIZENSHIP

I

THE MOST outstanding feature of external history in the century following the final overthrow of Greece (146 B.C.) was the spread of Roman rule over the whole Mediterranean basin. The African territory of Carthage was taken over in the same year; Spain was systematically pacified; an original occupation of Provence was extended to the whole of France, including the Low Countries as far as the Rhine; Asia Minor and Syria fell piecemeal; and Egypt was established as an open protectorate. Except for later frontier adjustments and strategic extensions of influence, the Roman dominion assumed in broad outline the shape it was going to retain for many centuries to come. This meant that a huge, conglomerate mass of countries and races came under the direct rule of a single Power, and all were united into a single system of administration. Furthermore, they were all given the same general mode of existence, and the form that this mode took was inevitably based on Hellenism. Despite its decadence, the outward form of Hellenistic life had infinite advantages over the uncivilized habits of the West and

North, and was necessarily bound to supersede them. The same spread of civilization that had ensued upon the conquests of Alexander the Great took place again, but this time in a westerly direction.

This was the first and most obvious result of Roman conquest. New races were given the benefit of Greek discovery and invention, and new territories were opened up to play their part in world development. The effects in all spheres of life were keenly felt, and as time allowed deeper assimilation, they became more and more important. Greek works of art and literature, Greek science and philosophy, Greek architecture, decoration and domestic appliances gained a universal currency, and one general standard of culture reigned everywhere. The natives of North Africa, Spain and France, as well as the Italians themselves, copied the material accomplishment of the Eastern Mediterranean, and naturally gained their own proficiency with the years. But, important as this was in itself, it had strict limitations. Hellenism, as such, was already a dying force, and nothing could revivify it. As we have seen in a previous chapter, it continued to move forward merely from the tremendous impetus it had received at the start, and had long since ceased to be itself an originating factor. Although it could spread over the whole Mediterranean and beyond, and though it transformed the mental habits of millions of Roman subjects, it could no longer produce anything new from its own resources, and the effects it did produce were but the shadow of the former triumph. The aspects of later civilization which owed their inception solely to the spreading of Hellenism were therefore but pale reproductions of classical prototypes, and even the literature of Rome itself, which was to impose on generations of mankind, was almost wholly an imitative thing.

More important from the point of view of this phase of our analysis is a second impulse proceeding from the Roman conquest, which was responsible for a new feature in the spreading civilization, and which entitles us to call it Græco-Roman. It will already have been observed that the feats of Roman arms were quite prodigious, and inevitably the impression they made on contemporaries was even more profound than that they make on us today. For centuries Rome had proved invincible, and there was apparently no limit to her growing power. Wherever she turned, she conquered, and the roll of subjugated nations continued yearly to expand. Moreover, when the Romans came, they came to stay. They brought with them a system of provincial administration, worked out through years of experience, and a military organization that made rebellion hopeless and foreign invasion impossible. To oust the Romans once they had set foot in a country was as difficult as to bar their original entry. Opposition was futile, and the advance of Rome was like the march of fate.

Although the tendency of the Romans to exploit their newly conquered provinces died hard, and for many years the provincials suffered oppression without means of redress, gradually a consciousness of the obligations they owed to the people under their jurisdiction awakened in the Romans, and a continuous process of amelioration began. We have already seen the system of gradual enfranchisement that had been applied so successfully in Italy, and despite a temporary lapse, they began to operate a similar system throughout the whole Roman world. With something in return for their lost independence, the provincials soon proceeded to assume a different attitude towards their conquerors, and the might of Rome, that had once been a thing of dread and dismay, became instead an object of awe and intense admiration. From being a mere military colossus, Rome emerged as the protector of civilization and the guarantee of future security, and an ever-present fear of despotism and war was removed from a world grown old in trepidation.

2

The immense improvement in the general morale over a wide area of the earth's surface that proceeded from this assurance can now be fully realized. From the Straits of Gibraltar to the banks of the Euphrates, from the beaches of Normandy to the oases of Cyrenaica, the "Pax Romana" prevailed uninterruptedly, and up to two hundred millions of people went about their daily tasks in the confident knowledge that their world was safe, permanent and progressive. They had an established order which assured stability, and all were joined in a common bond of fellowship, so that men of different race and tongue could greet one another as members of the same civilization. It is no wonder that they came to view the "Fortune" of Rome as something divine, and worshipped it as the expression of all their hopes of earthly success, since the psychological effect was quite overwhelming. At last men had something in which they could believe implicitly, something firm and immutable on which they could

C (H.H.T.)

pin their deepest faith, and a rooted belief of this sort acted as a background to the whole of their mental outlook. Rome had automatically infused some of her own moral strength into all the nations she conquered.

We thus see how Rome's material success gave a moral fillip to the ancient world, and the outward signs of it were not long in making their appearance. A prosperity came to reign over industry and commerce for two centuries such as history had never before recorded. Men had both the incentive and the stable conditions which trade requires, and their methods of organization reached an unprecedented height of development. Administration, finance, communications and civic amenities were brought to a new pitch of perfection, and objects of art and literature everywhere completed a splendid civilization. Although the standards of taste were Greek, the energy and stability were Roman. The Roman virtues of physical strength, determination and "guts" were added to the Hellenic ideals of intellectual and æsthetic expression, and the whole battery of ambition was concentrated in a new ideal which we can only call Græco-Roman. The outward sign of this ideal was the status of Roman citizenship, and, as we have seen, Roman policy gradually opened the way to its attainment. This became the aim of everybody in western and southern Europe and on the opposite shore of the Mediterranean, and all their dreams of earthly prosperity took rise from this one symbol of human completeness. Admission to the Roman citizenship was entry into the most privileged class on earth, for whose sake society itself was ordered, and the door was opened to the highest and best that life could offer.

In this way a whole world became united in purpose, and the ideals of Romans and non-Romans alike became identified in the precious citizenship. Of the effects of this idealism some notice has already been given, but we cannot judge it in detail until we know more precisely what were the privileges that Roman citizenship brought with it, and what were the qualities that constituted the ideal. As we have seen, an ideal is the form taken by a want or desire in some actual situation, when the creative imagination has given an emotional pattern to the ingredients of that situation, and therefore the effectiveness of the idealism centred round Roman citizenship could be only in proportion to the actual prerogatives of citizen-status and the actual character that it assumed.

For this reason, the form that the Romans gave to their own

status is of paramount importance at this period, and the whole course of a world's mental development depended on the final answer that the Romans found to the problem of their own ideological expression. The Romans ruled the civilized world: they were the arbiters of its fortunes. Now we find they were its mentors too, and would decide its spiritual future.

3

We saw in a previous chapter that the internal status of the Romans, both politically and socially, was still in course of evolution during the period of the Great Wars, and that the wars themselves produced certain important repercussions which were not so far contested; but when Rome came closely into contact with Hellenistic civilization in the first half of the 2nd century B.C., the reaction was instantaneous and the speed of evolution inescapably quickened. Just as Rome wrought immense changes in the kingdoms of the Eastern Mediterranean, so the reciprocal influence of Greek thought on the staid Romans was equally far-reaching, and in the hundred years beginning 133 B.C. a profound change came over Roman political life. Greek powers of analysis and Greek modes of thinking crystallized the vague Roman aspirations and brought to the surface the different currents of Roman opinion, and a conflict began in which the various elements in Roman society sought to impose their views on the format of the Roman State. This struggle commenced in Rome, and always had its centre of gravity there, but it spread over the whole Roman world, and was fought out with devastating bitterness from the uplands of central Spain to the shimmering strand of Alexandria. All the subjects of the Roman dominion throughout the Mediterranean followed the course of the conflict as helpless but intimate participants of the fighting, and awaited the result with closest interest. Even so, they did not understand its deepest implications. For on the outcome of this struggle depended the whole development of the Roman constitution and Roman society, and therefore of the form and status that Roman citizenship would bring with it, when the boon of enfranchisement spread to incorporate the rest.

4

Thus although the Romans by their conquests in the last two centuries before the birth of Christ carried Græco-Roman civilization to vast new territories of Europe and

Africa, and history broadens to include them, the clue to that history is to be sought solely in the Forum and Senate-House of Rome, and the whole of its subsequent development hinges on the details of Rome's internal politics during the century beginning 133 B.C. Our analysis of ancient history must therefore henceforward confine itself to the one subject of internal Rome, if we would find out the events and factors leading up to the final constitution of Roman citizenship, and we can only discover the aims and attitudes of the whole Roman world which was motivated by this ideal of citizenship if we follow the progress of the Romans in working out their own domestic and national problems. Thus when we have considered England's contribution to modern development, we will review the course of Roman politics from 133 B.C. onwards, as being at the same time the crux and a representation in miniature of the general history of this epoch.

CHAPTER IX

INDUSTRIALISM

I

In Chapter V we saw that the main problems facing the monarchies of 18th-century Europe were those connected with a rising population. The vigorous development of the 16th and 17th centuries had stimulated human fertility, and the ranks of the peasants in particular had been increased to an extent that put their very subsistence in jeopardy. It was a situation that demanded drastic action if disaster was to be avoided, yet the established order showed neither the ingenuity nor the will-power necessary to discover the means of meeting it, and instead, being deep in the sloth of decadence, frivolously left a seething mass of discontent to take care of itself.

Nor was the problem only that of their feeding and employment. There was also the urgency of their incorporation into the structure of society. The peasants were discovering from the works of Rousseau and others that they were human beings no less than their overlords, and were beginning to murmur at the degradation into which autocratic government had cast them. An incipient demand for the "Rights of Man" was heard as a vague rumble, breaking harshly in upon the

68

elegant harmonies of polite society, and crude forcefulness was lamentably ruffling the serene tenor of the age. The hour of retribution was fast approaching, and not all the wisdom and forbearance of Rousseau himself could have staved it off. For theory and reform were not enough. The first part of the solution had to be physical, practical and material. Food and wealth were the crying needs of the day, and no mere re-distribution of existing supplies would appease them, as those supplies were palpably inadequate. New sources were im-perative. Yet the continent of Europe had ceased to be pro-gressive, and its decadence gave no hope that they would be found. Its ideas had failed and its ingenuity was stifled.

This, then, was the situation that gave England her chance and that English activity was quick to utilize. In England, freedom of thought and freedom of expression had been fought for and won, and the Renaissance impulse towards humanist development had been fruitfully directed by an over-riding moral sense and had continued to progress, especially in the sphere of scientific investigation. The processes of thought and language were rationalized by a succession of brilliant intellects—Hobbes, Locke, Berkeley and Hume—and the re-discovery of Greek physics and mathe-matics restored sanity to the interpretation of natural phen-omena. Moreover, English practicality gave a new direction to science that Greek theorizing had never conceived, and Baconian induction and the experimental attitude that was so violently repressed on the Continent turned investigation into new utilitarian channels.

Scientific theory was applied to the solution of practical problems, until at length mechanical invention resulted. From the middle of the 18th century—Watt's introduction of steam-power in 1769 was the real beginning—there followed a series of inventions which changed the whole aspect of the productivity of human labour, and opened up completely unimagined sources of wealth. Machine succeeded machine, which enabled textiles and domestic appliances to be manu-factured in quantities and at prices which sufficed for the needs of everyone, and with the application of steam-power to locomotion, both on land and sea, these manufactures were spread about in a limitless profusion wherever demand existed. Meanwhile, the new command of organization and method wholly transformed the business of food-supply, and when home production, despite immense strides, failed to keep pace with the multiplying population, foreign foodstuffs were imported on a scale that made census increases irrelevant.

In this way not only was the problem of subsistence resolved, but also the elements of a solution were provided for the social aspect of the 18th-century dilemma. The practical men of England, having equipped themselves with the mechanical means of production, had evolved the factory system to exploit it, and the process began that is known to us as the "Industrial Revolution". The swelling population was absorbed into the new industries as quickly as it emerged, and new wealth and employment were found which closed the gap in the national economy, and opened the way to the social betterment of the depressed classes of society. Though fresh problems were started, the special 18th-century one was solved, and lack of the prime necessities of life, so far as their existence and not their distribution were concerned, never needed to trouble the world again.

2

The rewards of this English inventiveness were immediate and full. By 1760 the strategy of Chatham had already made her mistress of the seas, and as the only industrial nation in the world for many decades to come, she was able to export her manufactures to every continent and every land. Wealth accrued beyond the wildest dreams of avarice, and continental standards of income were made to seem ludicrously primitive. Everywhere from China to Peru, from Greenland to the Cape, British ships, carrying British goods or British raw materials, busily plied their trade, welcome, secure and uninterrupted, whilst at home great new towns and cities were springing up almost overnight to make yet more goods and metamorphose yet more raw materials. Over wide areas of Great Britain, what had once been wood and meadow-land became in half a century forested with stark mill-chimneys and furrowed with endless rows of cottages. Industrialization seemed the perfect answer for everything.

And yet it was not the industrial system alone that was responsible for British success. Without the tremendous enterprise that Britons exhibited and the intense exertions they put forward, this miracle of manufacturing would never have been performed. They worked hard and long, and were as unsparing of themselves as of their labour. Once more it was the nice balance of individual and communal effort under the prevailing conditions that was the deciding factor, and the combination of personal and patriotic motives that gave the boundless incentive to action. The English had worked out a system of government that gave the maximum of individual liberty and the minimum of public interference, so that private enterprise had all the scope it needed for commercial development, and it was not slow to seize its golden opportunity; but at the same time they had a sense of patriotism, and their leaders a tradition of service, that never ceased to combine national advantage with personal gain, and what one section of the community sought for its own remuneration, another consolidated for the general benefit. Thus the commercial supremacy that individual effort had created was followed up by national concern, and the public security was assured, if necessary, by force of arms. The history of the East India Company in this period is typical of British development in which private commercial interests were gradually merged into imperial and it illustrates the slow transition that built the second British Empire (with the first we must deal later) and transformed it by easy stages from a mere marketing system into a Commonwealth of Nations.

There was another way in which the liberal principles of the English system of government contributed to this success, and that was its ability to assimilate by degrees not only the new industrial interests, but also the new industrial classes. For the rising manufacturing districts brought forth fresh strata into society—employers soaring on the gale of prosperity, and employees only just escaping the worst effects of overpopulation on subsistence wages—and both were foreign to the established order. But we have seen how in previous generations English society and English government had ever broadened in time of need and adapted themselves to new circumstances without violence to old tradition, and in the century between 1760 and 1867 they did so again. There were new standards of wealth and of poverty alike which seemed at moments to threaten the very foundations of national unity and bid fair to subvert the basic understanding of the years, but in the long run morale held, and the Constitution stood firm through all the trials of a social upheaval. The country changed, too, from a territorial to a financial system of reckoning, but a *modus operandi* was worked out which incorporated the new attitude within the framework of the old presuppositions.

Thus, whilst maintaining the order and organization necessary for the utmost exploitation of the new industrialism, the people of England also found a use and a niche for the growing masses in their midst which were being excluded and repressed on the Continent, and a temporary outlet was provided for their demand for expression which, as we have seen, was contributing greatly to the continental *impasse*. This particular feature is so important that we must consider it again later in more detail, but for the moment it will suffice to observe how efficacious it was in clinching the success of the Industrial Revolution in England. English idealism stood firmly in its place, and the moral strength it inspired proved wholly beyond price.

3

Industrialism was thus the way in which England absorbed both the energy and the enthusiasm of the new masses of people that 17th- and 18th-century expansion had brought with it, and by broadening her basis of government she likewise absorbed industrialism. The commercial success that resulted was so marked, and her imperial power became so great, that every corner of the world felt the repercussions and every nation was eventually bound to take notice. In Europe the effect was soon only less profound than in England itself, and the new English inventions began to find ready homes, particularly in France, Germany and the Low Countries, and to a lesser extent elsewhere. Mills started to rise at every suitable point on the Continent, and big industrial areas spread out their grime and smoke wherever coalfields facilitated their development. Europe became mechanically-minded, and manufacturing began to change its outward appearance as effectively as that of England. Industrialism had arrived, and was henceforth to be an essential part of Western civilization.

The internal results, too, that accrued from this transformation were similar to those that had occurred in England. The growing populations were largely catered for, and given a place and an interest in society: new wealth was created which paved the way for a solution of the economic and social problems of the day; and a fresh incentive was provided both for individual and national endeavour. The vast stirring that had culminated in the French Revolution, and was heading merely for chaos from lack of tangible objectives, was given direction and purpose, and the latent ardour that neither decadent monarchism nor the naturalism of Rousseau could fertilize sprang fruitfully to life in the kindlier soil of material

72

betterment. It was a new Renaissance, with scientific discovery supplying the machinery that was needed for progress and giving the means of expression to the vague aspirations of millions—aspirations which now crystallized and held relevance to the actual conditions of the world. English practicality had saved civilization from the wilderness of abstractions, and Europe was once again galvanized into useful action.

The moral impulse that proceeded from this sudden access of enthusiasm was sufficient to restore the debilitated powers of a whole continent. The Western European countries as well as their overseas colonies began to show the energy and enterprise which spread broadcast the deepest effects of Western civilization and seemed to establish finally the racial superiority of the white man. Moreover, as we have seen, the feeling for "natural rights" that Rousseau had inculcated was at last given something it could grasp. At the same time as new wealth accumulated which could eventually raise the standard of living, a material incentive was provided, both for personal and corporate effort, which gave all classes of society a fresh outlook on the function of the State. A new spirit of nationalism was generated that changed the whole aspect of Europe. Ambition was reborn both for self and for country, and the ardour that 18th-century monarchy had been unable either to use or engender found a new outlet in a wider internal co-operation. Politics also began to progress.

4

The comparison with the ancient world will now be clear. The material success of Great Britain infused a new moral strength and supplied new ways and means for the regeneration of a complete civilization. This was just what Rome had done, and the new mode of living also was coloured with the external innovations of the dominant Power in a closely similar manner. Degenerate society embraced the proffered opportunities, and found in them the means of creating new ideals which gave the spur to yet further endeavour and produced, if not a unity of interest, at least an identity of aim. Spiritual bankruptcy gave place to boundless enthusiasm.

Moreover, the increasing improvement of communications, and the more rapid spread of industry and Western habits it facilitated, carried the effects farther and farther afield, until by the 20th century every continent was sharing in this surge of material progress and took on readily the external

C 2

appurtenances of Western civilization. Just as Rome had instigated the forward movement of the whole ancient world, so did industrialism the modern, and our history broadens continuously, until it embraces the whole of the habitable earth. European civilization becomes world civilization, and every land and race henceforward plays its part in the political and economic whole. The ramifications of commerce and industry spread even deeper and wider, so that the mutual interdependence of classes and nations grew progressively greater, and major events which happened in one part of the globe and to one section of society, inevitably brought their reactions everywhere and to everybody else.

Unfortunately, there is no short-cut to the understanding of this world-wide history such as we found in the Roman age, and whereas we shall be able to follow the general course of the last century B.C. within the single subject of Roman internal politics, the modern world has not been under the direction of a single political unit, but has had to work out its own problems when and wherever they arose. And so we, too, must follow them whithersoever they lead us. But now more than ever, the value of the ancient comparison will make itself apparent, as we shall have before us a counterpart to modern times displayed briefly and succinctly within the compass of a single narrow stage, and the conflict of ideas which we shall see played out in the Forum of Rome will serve to focus our attention to the important features of the conflicts of modern Europe and elsewhere. We shall, in fact, be able to pick out the long threads which hold together the larger pattern by virtue of what happened in the previous epoch. For just as Greek thinking accelerated the *dénouement* of Roman political development and enabled all sections of the State to crystallize their views and aspirations, so the scientific outlook of the 18th and 19th centuries brought to a head the powerful forces that were gathering in European society, and flung the whole world into the maelstrom of nationalist and class warfare that have signalized our 20th century.

To elucidate the causes of this unprecedented strife, and to seek to uncover the things for which men have fought and are still fighting, must be our next purpose. We shall find that in the modern world of 1760 onwards it is the nature and effectiveness of men's ideals which have moulded the main course of history, just as did the ideal of Roman citizenship 2,000 years before, and in the same manner that we must discover the fundamental objectives of Græco-Roman idealism to understand its history, so must we explore the motives which have brought our civilization to its present stage, to see its meaning. Only when we have done that shall we be in a position to assess the value and coerciveness of the ideals that move us today.

CHAPTER X

REVOLUTIONARY ROME

I

WHEN LAST we considered the political situation at Rome about the middle of the 2nd century B.C., we found that though the Roman State was in theory a democracy in which equality of political opportunity had been established by law, there had in fact been a drastic narrowing of the Government to meet the demands of a century of almost continuous warfare. The fortunes of the country were being directed almost exclusively by a small clique of privileged families, and these alone filled the higher executive posts and supplied the members of the *de facto* legislative assembly. No direct legislation had been used to bring about this decisive modification of the constitution, but it was solely the result of a long process of minor changes in procedure, each of which had been adopted to meet some particular situation and had passed almost unnoticed into the tradition of later years. The success that attended the Senate's direction of affairs was more than sufficient justification for it, and the selfless service which individual senators devoted to the State completely reassured those who gave them this authority. The Senate's position, therefore, however unofficial, was never seriously contested throughout the period of the Great Wars against Carthage and Macedon, and all classes of society were more than content to leave things in such competent hands for the duration.

With the close of the period of life-and-death struggle, however, there came a profound change in outlook. A demand was raised, more and more insistently, that the emergency powers of the Senate should be relaxed, now that the emergency for which they were designed to cater was over, and that the equalitarian principles of the theoretical democracy should be reaffirmed and established in actual practice.

A new generation of nobles, however, had grown up in the exercise of authority, who were reluctant to part with it. Authority, in addition to its own distinctions, had now many perquisites since the wars of conquest, and life for the privileged classes was far from the simple existence it had been in pre-war days. Besides the lion's share of actual plunder that a successful campaign brought the commander-in-chief and his officers, there were many lucrative posts to be had in the occupied territories, and there were also important judicial functions at Rome which not only brought their own rewards, but also assured their permanence. The contact with Eastern Mediterranean countries, too, had given the possession of money an entirely new significance and made it for the first time a *sine qua non* of the "good life". For, owing to their long-standing war-time economies, the Romans had never of their own accord either considered or had opportunity for the refinements of civilization, and had lived in a primitive state of thrift and improvisation that accorded fully with their military record; but now, coming suddenly face to face with the luxury and extravagance of the Hellenistic world, they realized only too well the delights they had foregone, and seized on them with a verve which screamed their desire to make up for lost time. Money was the key that opened the gate to this golden wonderland, and money became the urgent need of every self-respecting Roman. There was thus little likelihood that the nobles would surrender lightly the glowing chances of its acquisition that office and preferment gave them, and a period of controversy was inevitable.

This determination was strengthened by the fact that members of the Senate did not participate in trade. They had themselves passed a law forbidding it, in order to exclude from the Government the many wealthy merchants who were aspiring to senatorial rank, and, in any case, they affected to despise commerce as beneath the dignity of soldiers and statesmen. They refused to give anything in return for their monetary acquisitions but their military and political services. Whilst these services were of a high order and devoted to the national advantage all went well, but unfortunately the depravity of Greece cast a fatal spell over the inexperienced Romans and turned their creditable ambition to less creditable self-indulgence. Their quest for glory became mere acquisitiveness, and their ability suffered from the worst effects of

76

lack of concentration and over-presumptuousness. Senatorial government deteriorated to senatorial misgovernment, and both political and military affairs began to go wrong.

Face to face with the nobility, there were two main classes in society who began to raise the voice of disapproval. One was the growing commercial community against whom discriminating legislation had already been passed, and included the middle classes generally; the other was the mass of artisans and labourers who constituted the vast majority of the city population. Both had demands of their own on the Government, and if their demands had been given a hearing, both were at first willing to respect its immense prestige, but when they met with nothing but senatorial obstruction, they began to reconsider their attitude and to devise other means of obtaining their desires. The Senate's position was already vulnerable, since its power was based not in strict law, but on a complicated system of accumulated precedents, and it was protected only by the Romans' respect for age-long custom. Thus when Greek rationalism began to dissolve something of the halo that surrounded mere tradition, the excluded parties prepared to storm the Senate's authority and to implement the legal democracy.

There thus emerged three distinct political parties in Roman domestic affairs, each with its own party programme and each concerned to impose its own views on the national policy. At the top was the Senatorial party, strong in its long history of achievement and in its actual possession of the reins of government; next came the commercial and middle classes, loosely lumped together as the "Equites" or knights, who wielded the immense power of untold wealth and were anxious for beneficial legislation to further their commercial enterprises as well as to share in the honours of office; and lastly, the working-classes, the "Popular" party, who had lost their livelihoods through long years of soldiering and were sunk in the degradation of unemployment and poverty; social and economic alleviation were their demands and some sort of security for the future. This, then, was the raw material from which the final drama of the Roman Republic was to be composed, and which provided the setting for the culminating heroics of the 1st century B.C.

2

The first shock to the constitution came in the year 133 B.C. A genuine and disinterested attempt to improve the parlous

77

condition of Italian agriculture was allowed to deteriorate into a political crisis of the most ominous kind, and blood was shed for the first time in Roman constitutional history. What governmental inertia had begun, radical impetuosity completed, with neither side sensing the fatal direction in which things were drifting.

It happened in the following way. The reformer, Tiberius Gracchus, was a young noble of liberal views, concerned only to bring back some measure of prosperity to the country-side of his affections, but this could not be done without State interference in the sacred rights of private property, and that, too, the most basic of all properties—land. Now, the Senators were above all things great landowners, and this was touching them on their most sensitive spot. Their immediate reaction was to apply certain obstructive practices in Roman constitutional procedure, and by dint of these they successfully contrived to block the proposals. Gracchus, however, had staked his career on the reforms, and rallying the Popular party to his aid, he sought to by-pass the Government by an unconventional appeal to the legalities of the theoretical democracy. Government partisans rushed to arms in alleged defence of the constitution, and in the ensuing turbulence Gracchus was stabbed and bludgeoned to death. Senatorial authority was indeed reasserted, but in a manner that left much misgiving.

More far-reaching still were the motions tabled ten years later by Tiberius' brother, Gaius. He had learned the lessons of his brother's failure, and saw that the Senate's position was not to be assailed except by an all-party alliance. In addition to re-introducing the same agricultural reforms, therefore, he drew up an attractive programme of legislation that would put both the middle and lower classes solidly behind him, and sponsored a number of bills which were designed to remove their immediate grievances. At the same time he armed himself with a counter-blast to the Senate's obstructional tactics, and by dint of much strenuous canvassing managed to get his proposals passed into law. The Government was only biding its time, however, and eighteen months later, in 121 B.C., when the first public enthusiasm was over, it was emboldened to make a general attack on the legality of the reforms. Gaius Gracchus responded with the same rash impulsiveness as his brother; disrespect for the conventional procedure led to a breach of the peace; and the Government eventually found the pretext it wanted for a recourse to arms. C. Gracchus thus met his death at the hands of political opponents, armed by a Government which knew no other protection for itself or the public security.

Once again the Senate had blustered its way through and mastered a menacing situation, but much of C. Gracchus' legislation remained in force, and the opposition parties had moreover gained a new consciousness of their own individuality which boded ill for the future. Nor did the Senate make politic use of the breathing-space it had won for itself. Instead, Governmental incapacity was allowed to show itself in yet another sphere of State—one, indeed, on which it founded its strongest claim to authority—namely, that of military affairs. A border war against a local chieftain in Algeria was conducted with such manifestations of incompetence and corruption that the Roman forces even seemed in danger of being driven out of Tunis as well. To make matters worse, a genuine danger was gathering in the North, where a periodic migration of barbarians threatened to break into Italy itself; and yet the Senate proved quite incapable of finishing off the war in Africa, let alone of making the strenuous exertions that the other situation demanded. Meanwhile, it was common knowledge that the most talented soldier of the day was one C. Marius, but as he was a commoner who had risen from the ranks, the Senate haughtily refused to employ him, and muddled along instead with their own second-rate commanders, who proceeded to lose battle after battle. This gave the opposition parties the chance they had been waiting for, and over the heads of the Government they combined to force through a bill appointing Marius to the post of commander-in-chief. At once Marius overhauled the whole military organization, and in two short but brilliant campaigns first restored the position in North Africa, and then utterly smashed the barbarian hordes in the North.

The Popular party was exultant, as well it might be, and on the strength of its triumph proceeded to promote a mass of legislation which would make permanent its ascendancy. Its excesses, however, soon alienated the middle classes, who swung over to the side of the Senate, and after a period of turbulence, the nobility regained their wonted authority. This authority was strengthened for the moment by another crisis inside Italy, when in the year 91 B.C. a serious rebellion broke out amongst the Italians in the South, and this time the Senate managed to produce a military genius from its own ranks. L. Cornelius Sulla, a blue-blooded aristocrat, was

79

instrumental in restoring order both in Italy and in Rome, and gave back to the Senate some of its sinking prestige. But the moment he had turned his back to attend to a fresh war that broke out in the East, the Popular party renewed its attacks on the Government, and in 87 B.C. completely carried the day.

By this time passions had become so inflamed, and unruliness had grown to be such a recognized concomitant of political controversy, that the victory of the Popular party was the signal for an outbreak of violence and venom such as Roman politics had never before witnessed. Aristocrats were murdered on their own doorsteps, and their families driven callously out of the city; civic administration came to a standstill; and politics developed into a tragic farce. Yet even this anarchy was mild compared with the cold-blooded and comprehensive purge of democratic personalities that was carried out by Sulla on the Senate's behalf, when in 82 B.C. he returned with a victorious army from Asia Minor and used his forces to impose a reconstituted Senatorial government on the Roman Republic. Sulla was nothing if not thorough, and to allow his new constitution time to settle in, he determined on a ruthless extermination of all actual and possible opponents who might attack the legal foundation that he gave to senatorial rule. The force of law which mere tradition lacked, he himself would supply, and woe to the unfortunate who chose to resist him. Aristocratic government was to be reaffirmed once and for all, and the decimated middle and lower classes had only just enough strength left to signify their grudging assent.

3

The details of this fifty years of turmoil are less important to our purposes than the general tendency they illustrate. It is evident that new forces were at work in Roman history which it was beyond the means of Roman experience to accommodate, and political bankruptcy had resulted. Feelings had hardened to such a degree that the spirit of co-operation had withered, and Sulla's reforms did no more than solve the riddle of the constitutional knot by cutting it. Our task is to elucidate these new factors and consider the reasons for the shortcomings they uncovered in Roman political character.

Political controversy itself was no new thing in Roman history. On the contrary, the democracy of 287 B.C. had only been established by dint of century-long argument and counter-argument between the aristocracy and the common people. What was certainly new was the violence and bitterness with which it was conducted. The strongest weapon in the old days had been general strikes, but these had been carried out with a due sense of responsibility and feeling for the gravity of the situation that had never let it get out of hand, and a compromise had always been reached eventually. But now neither side was willing to mitigate one tittle of its demands, nor denied the use of any means to accomplish them, regardless of the ultimate consequences. Something very drastic had happened to destroy the old restraint.

The external conditions which led to the emergence of the three political parties have already been adumbrated, and we saw that the immediate cause of their antagonism was the intransigeant attitude of the nobility. Under the influence of Hellenistic standards of opulence, the Senatorial order was interested only to extract the maximum enjoyment of which their newly aroused appetites were capable, and they had ceased to give care and attention to the business of State as their conscientious forbears had done. Their training was no longer the hard one of discipline and service, and arrogance displaced the virtues of submission to authority. Contact was thus lost both with the needs of the country and the welfare of the people, till at length an attitude of overbearing contempt disfigured their whole relations with other Romans.

In the light of our previous investigations, we can classify this change as a decay in moral idealism. The rewards of success had come to have a greater importance than the winning of them, and the material benefits of power had completely overwhelmed the moral impulse that makes for its achievement. The aristocrats still showed the old vigour and determination: they still had the same physical courage and singleness of mind; but they applied themselves to different objects than formerly, and those objects did not conduce to the general welfare. They took over as their new ideal the luxurious and extravagant living that the depraved ingenuity of Greece had produced, without any of the beneficent safeguards of Greek thought and philosophy, and the material effects of degenerate Hellenism were wholly theirs, intensified, however, by Roman thoroughness.

Such mode of life was to be the splendid reward of noble pre-eminence, and in its decadence the Senatorial order considered itself alone deserving, alone fit to rule and bear the prize of success. Such mode of life, too, could only be maintained at the expense of others, and to secure it a world must be enslaved. Co-operation with other classes was thus as impossible as it was undesirable, and to their blunted sensibilities the ethics of society could extend no farther than their own immediate coterie. In the old days the resources of the State and the rich increase that military success brought with it had redounded to the advantage of the whole community, but now they benefited one class only, the nobility, who resented any suggestion that the State should assist its less fortunate members. The State was represented by the Senate, and to the Senate the State should belong. All other classes were merely essential ingredients who worked for the welfare of its brightest ornament, the Government, and their reward was the pittance that the voracious appetites of the nobility could allow them. There was thus an identification of one party with the whole State, and revolution was made the only road for reformers. This was the blank wall that forced the opposition parties into their dilemma.

When we consider the behaviour of the opposition parties in their unwelcome position, we find that the line of action they followed in no way alleviated it. On the contrary, both the middle and lower classes showed a tendency to disregard the principles of government and the safeguards of national security in a way that went far to justify the Senate's exclusiveness and could, therefore, only react to their own detriment.

Let us take first the Popular party. From the start their leaders eschewed a policy of conciliation, and made no attempt to set an example of rigid constitutionalism which might hope to gain adherents in conservative quarters. The urgency of the need for public assistance blinded them to the need for care of the State as a whole, and they were willing to risk chaos for a prospect of immediate reform. Granted, moreover, that revolutionary procedure was the only course open to them as a result of Senatorial obstinacy, they nevertheless proved themselves completely without an effective programme of their own, and had nothing to put in the place of the old Senatorial Government they aimed to remove. Their original legislation was merely palliative, and their later openly subversive. At no time did they see to the root of the trouble, and they were concerned only to obtain economic redress, without considering political or social cause and effect. Their periods of government thus meant merely anarchy, and they succeeded even less than the hide-bound Senate in furthering the public welfare, or even their own.

The reasons for this will be apparent. Unemployment and degradation had sapped the moral strength of the city populace; poverty and starvation were making it desperate. The conditions under which most of them lived were something new in Roman history, and from year to year were growing steadily worse. As the population of the city increased, the overcrowding produced the foulest of slums, and under-nourishment in the enclosed urban quarters led to disease and enervation which finally broke the standard of morality. Nor was the situation improved by the growing contrast with the state of display maintained by the rich. As the poor got poorer, the wealth of the upper classes increased by leaps and bounds, and their taste for extravagance made it more and more blatant. Two reactions inevitably followed amongst the poor—one of blind hate, which vented itself in moments of ascendancy, and the other of parasitical subservience, which fawned on the wealthy at other times and accepted their haughty patronage. They were thus rendered wholly un-reliable, and could be suborned from any consistent action by promises and bribes. Their leaders were swept to extremes in success and left impotent in defeat.

To such people the only remedial measures likely to be attractive were those that produced immediate results, and no long-term programme of social reform was ever supported that might have got to the bottom of the trouble. Palliatives thus remained the stock-in-trade of politicians of every political colour. Public works were undertaken on an in-creasing scale, as well as sporadic attempts to resettle the land, which did something to put money in circulation; but the chief stand-by, an innovation of C. Gracchus, was the regulation of food-prices by means of treasury subsidies, so as to bring the staple items of poor-class diet within the reach of the most poverty-stricken. This was a bold expedient that proved so popular that its continuance under the Senatorial regime was assured, and we shall have cause to consider it in much greater detail later. For the moment, it is important to observe its social and economic inadequacy, even though it meant that the State had been forced to admit some measure of responsibility for the welfare of its humblest constituents—and that, too, in an age of the grossest individualism.

This character of individualism was most decisively ex-emplified by the Equites or middle classes. We have seen

83

how they were excluded from the Government, in spite of their growing wealth, and the result was to force them more than ever into concentration on their own commercial enterprises. Many of them became large-scale employers of sweated labour, monopolists of the most anti-social kind, and financiers without a single human feeling. They were interested only in the accumulation of capital, which they used ruthlessly and for their own purposes, and their patriotism looked to the State only for good business and legal backing. Government or misgovernment was the same to them so long as their financial interests were not adversely affected, and any sort of social conscience was the last thing to be expected from them. They threw their vast influence first one way and then the other, according as they could expect financial benefit, but they had no political programme of their own which might be calculated to repair the fallen fortunes of Roman republican development. They were, indeed, one of the worst products of the new spirit.

5

This, then, is the picture that we get of the motivating forces in Roman society during the half-century 133 B.C. to 81 B.C. The sudden access of wealth from the conquered territories had turned men's minds from the pursuit of the common good and violently upset the balance of individual and communal effort. Instead, men concentrated on their own personal advancement, and, losing their feeling for their countrymen as a whole, became conscious only of their own particular class. The accumulation of wealth that followed, and the accompanying poverty its maldistribution made inevitable, served merely to aggravate the position, and precipitated the failing morale into a new sort of materialism. The old values were finally lost.

We have seen how in both earlier and later societies the spirit of co-operation had been at times broken down and had developed into a pursuit of personal desires and aspirations, but this was something quite different. Whereas, in our previous examples there had always been some ideal of culture, however faded, to condition the way men thought, the Romans had no such tradition and no such ideal. Their scramble for wealth was merely to facilitate their taste for display, their urge for material comfort and their lust for power, and they banded together in cliques simply because the greater complexity of their world organization necessitated
84

it. Nor had their religion any virtues which might have made for restraint. A mere primitive totemism, without moral or spiritual value, it ceased almost completely to have significance, once a wider knowledge of the world had laid bare its shortcomings; and as soon as the patriotism that had been the strength of Rome collapsed before the onset of amassing wealth, they were left with nothing but the material things in life as the objects of their tremendous enthusiasm. Then, too, being so intensely practical, they applied new means and new measures to their pursuit which made the triumph only the greater and drove the malady only the deeper.

All classes in society were thereby affected, high by reason of their success, and low by reason of their failure, and civil dissension resulted, as we have seen. By 80 B.C. the use of physical violence had become open and avowed, and no side made any scruple about requisitioning the armed forces for the prosecution of its own acquisitive aims. In this revolutionary atmosphere the first round was won hands down by the nobility through the legions of Sulla, and Sulla himself hoped he had made permanent its ascendancy—with what grounds we shall see later. But at this point we must leave Roman history temporarily to consider the first stages of modern industrialized society.

CHAPTER XI

ROMANTIC REVOLUTION

I

During our review of 18th-century Europe we had occasion to observe from time to time the teaching of Jean Jacques Rousseau (1712–1778), the French prophet of modern democracy, and we must now consider in more detail the nature of the contributions he had made. He had brought into the open the new demand for expression that was beginning to stir the rising masses of the population, and had preached a new doctrine of sentiment that was conditioning its course. He taught that man was made, not to be the pawn of coldly calculating governments, but the glory of a common humanity, and that he possessed certain "natural rights" which the love of his fellow-men should willingly concede. The spirit of fraternity that he advocated crossed all the frontiers which the schemes of dynasts had erected, and took no account of age-old nationalist aspirations, striving boldly to awaken a fellow-feeling that would lead to world co-operation. It was new, startling in its imaginative reach, and alluring to a mass of depressed mankind. It became the sentiment on which the urge for social improvement was built up, and supplied the emotional content of the quest for political liberty. A vast movement was set on foot which turned politics in a new direction, revitalized art and literature in the "Romantic Revolt", and irradiated optimistic notions of perfectibility throughout the whole realm of human thought.

The immediate objective was independence of both external and internal despotism. Conquered peoples must be freed from the yoke of foreign oppression, and degraded nations must rise from the chains of their own despotic governments. All over Europe and wherever white men had settled themselves in any number democratic and independence movements sprang up, whose aim was to materialize the romance of that self-government, which would release the flow of the milk of human kindness. Meanwhile, the continental monarchies, as we have seen, were old and powerless to avoid the rising torrent of enthusiams, but mere inertia could accomplish one thing, and that was to do nothing. They did it signally. They dropped the ponderous bulk of their dead weight solidly in the way of any progress, and would rather the tide broke over them than that they themselves should move. For, being wholly bound by their traditions, they preferred extermination to life in a world they failed to understand, and prepared to die hard in the last ditch of reaction. Moreover, possessing the reins of government, they used all the resources of state at their command to protect themselves, and in the spirit of *L'Etat, c'est moi*, refused to recognize any other party as a legitimate organ of rule. There was a lack not only of the will to reform, but also of the machinery for it, and revolution became slowly but surely the only method of change.

We thus find that European society in the latter half of the 18th century possessed the same two factions that the Senate and Popular party had represented in Rome, and which were bound to clash through the unbending attitude of the Government. Yet the comparison does not end there. There was also a rising commercial community which played a similar half-way rôle to the Equites and had its own individual trade interests, identified neither with those of the democrats nor those of the monarchists. As yet it was not fully articulate, but in the early 19th century it found a voice and a dogma in the writings of Jeremy Bentham, the "Utilitarian", and began to exert its influence more and more. Its objective was a liberal type of government that was to do no more than provide the conditions suitable for trade and industry, and then not interfere any further in the running of things; and though participation in the Government would certainly help its own development, absolute democracy was not essential, and might even be inconvenient. On one main issue, however, they were united with the democrats, and that was in breaking down the exclusiveness of the old monarchical governments, and to this end, therefore, they prepared to co-operate for the time being.

How these combined assaults on the established order fared is the history of the hundred years beginning about 1750. The process took longer in the modern world than in Rome because more countries were engaged in it and the area involved was greater, but the general course is the same and the outcome almost as lamentable.

2

The first noteworthy success of the new movement came from a totally unexpected quarter. The valuable lessons which were to lead to the creation of the second British Empire had not yet been learned, and the first British Empire surprisingly gave the setting for a triumphant bid for independence. The Thirteen Colonies on the eastern seaboard of the North American continent had from the start been populated mainly by political and religious malcontents who preferred to carve out new destinies for themselves in an unknown land rather than surrender their principles to the needs of a settled life in England, and the pioneering conditions under which they lived served only to foster this love of independence. When they met what they construed as a lack of sympathy in the Home Government, therefore, they struck for their freedom, and in 1776 began to put into operation the new democratic principles in their republican-constituted United States of America. Their spirit was already tempered by the liberal tradition of English politics, and they had all of English practicality in the conduct of affairs, so that they made full use of their opportunity, and under the guiding hand of their immaculate George Washington successfully overcame the pitfalls of their early development.

Unfortunately, the British Government, being not yet at that time awakened to the spirit of the age, refused to accept the situation as it stood, took up a legal rather than an imaginative attitude, and made a feeble show of arms which did no more than estrange the official relations of the two countries for over a century. The birth of democracy was not allowed to come with songs of joy and pipes of peace. The rest of Europe and its colonies, however, were delighted—the "powers that were", because the pride of England had been humbled, and the commoners, because the "Rights of Man" had been affirmed and justified in fact—and both sides prepared to exploit the occasion to the full. In France the demand for reform gained fresh volume and gathered for open assault, but the Government on its part was all the more determined to withstand it. Feeling ran higher and higher, until at last in 1790 the storm broke and the Bourbons and their hangers-on were swept away in a flood of enthusiasm that knew no bar.

The effect of the French Revolution was electric. A tense feeling of expectancy throbbed in every youthful heart, and, as Wordsworth recorded, "it was bliss to be alive". The romantic principles of liberty, equality and fraternity were being given factual manifestation in one of the most powerful and densely populated nations of the Continent, and adherents in every land awaited impatiently the spread of the new gospel of love. It was a clean sweep, and all the tortuousness and callousness of traditional politics were to be consigned irrevocably to the flames where they belonged. But soon the flames enveloped more than the rotten timbers of a worn-out constitution, and Madame Guillotine began to levy an ominous toll of heads. The dawn of freedom had heralded but the day of terror, and a night was approaching that would fill the sky with the angry glow of war and pestilence and death. The official attitude of the neighbouring countries had from the first been one of reserve and aloofness, and soon the pretext was found to embark upon open hostilities: the Revolution, already reeling from its own excesses, was to be finally and utterly smashed. Yet, threatened on all sides, the French communists elicited from apparently nowhere a bond of union and national enthusiasm which rapidly chased their assailants headlong from the field; defence turned into a crusade, and finally burgeoned into a rampant militarism under the dictatorship of Napoleon which threatened to engulf the whole world. Scarcely did the strength of England and the intermittent help of her allies avail to bring the structure to the ground in twenty years of wars, and then only at a cost that was to cripple social and political progress for years.

For democracy had received a setback from which it seemed it might never recover. The golden visions that the very names of liberty, equality and fraternity had evoked had been broken by the Reign of Terror and scattered to the winds by the spectre of Napoleon, and the policy of conservatism stood confirmed and in arms. Vainly did Shelley, Keats and Schiller dash their sensibilities on the iron buffers of reaction. What the spirit of liberty could not effect on the grand scale, therefore, it had to attempt on a less, and the years following the Battle of Waterloo saw a series of minor revolts, riots and reform campaigns which met with varying degrees of success. Greece threw off the yoke of Turkey; the Spanish colonies of South America parted company with the mother-country; and in 1830 France finally got rid of the re-imposed Bourbons. But none of this was accomplished without blood and tears, and once again tempers gradually began to rise. England indeed passed her First Reform Bill in 1832, and so averted the worst of the danger, but only after a period of unparalleled agitation and as a result of the decisive intervention of the new industrial interests. In continental Europe, on the other hand, the cause of liberty remained desperate, and the reactionary powers of the Holy Alliance banded together to stifle and re-press every kind of racial, political and cultural liberty. Reformers took refuge in plots, assassinations and conspiracies which mocked at the outer prosperity of the times, and re-volution became a sinister reality to smiling Ruritania. The climax came in 1848, the "year of revolutions", when country after country struck for its independence and freedom, and a general conflagration seemed imminent. But the established governments were forewarned and forearmed, and risings in France, Italy, Hungary and elsewhere were put down with a thunder of guns that seemed to sound the knell of a better world. Rousseau might never have lived.

3

Mutatis mutandis, this is the story of Rome all over again. A move for political liberty that had begun with all the golden prospects which genuine enthusiasm could give it foundered on the rock of reactionary authority, and changed into a subversive undercurrent that threatened the very foundations of society. Yet authority exerted no effort to accommodate the new spirit or utilize its energy: it only redoubled its determination to supress it and uphold the worn-out customs of a former age. We are therefore justified in considering whether the reasons for this process are the same in the later as in the earlier epoch, and for this purpose we will examine in turn the three sections of society which played their parts in it.

First, the monarchical governments and their satellite aristocracies of birth. We have frequently had reason to observe that these were effete, nerveless and moribund, and that their potentiality for progress was nil. Their ideals had long ago been fully realised at the court of the *Roi Soleil*, and they had henceforward lost themselves in endless imitation. For the last time we will pay tribute to the accomplishments of their brief hey-day which had certainly been brilliant in the extreme. Literature and art had been given new standards of polish and gentility which could not but be beneficial in the long run, and architecture had been inspired to new heights of rational splendour. The whole aspect of life was softened and humanized in a manner for which civilization owes an inestimable debt, and Pope, Haydn and Fontainebleau were but the fairest of its products.

Yet the inspiration passed, and by the middle of the 18th century its main work was done. Europe was ready to move on towards a further goal and seek new modes of expression of a broader sort, even though the monarchical governments would not go with it. For these could not. Their scintillating manner of life depended wholly on perpetuation of the servile conditions to which their subjects were condemned, and they sought no opportunity for their emancipation. Continued autocracy had levied its toll on their humanity, and whilst they ceased to consider themselves even biologically related to the other classes of society, they did not perceive the parasitical nature of their own distinctive position. Their idealism had failed; their usefulness had gone; but their power unfortunately remained. And this power they were determined to exert to the full.

Like the Popular party at Rome, therefore, the democratic movements in Europe and America were faced with the alternative of repression or revolution; a smooth transition to a broader existence was ruled out and the goodwill that was essential for a compromise was precluded from the start. Once the fiercer passions were aroused, circumspection would vanish, and an era of trouble be rendered inevitable. In a similar dilemma our review of ancient Rome gave us cause to question the soundness of the tactics adopted by the Popular party, and if from this hint we consider the development of modern democracy, we regrettably find the same impulsiveness and the same hastiness of action that had spoiled its prospects in Rome. The French Revolution irrevocably set the tempo of the age, and even granted that the French revolutionaries had received disastrous provocation from both their own and foreign Governments, they failed signally to exercise the restraint that could alone have remedied the situation. The horrors of the September massacres and the guillotine inevitably alienated opinion everywhere, even before the wilful aggression of the Napoleonic era began. Despite the high precepts that were given effect in the new constitution of the Republic, there had arisen insuperable obstacles to tolerance and co-operation, and the love of fellow-men that Rousseau had prophesied to be the outcome of liberal government failed completely to materialize.

As we have already seen, mere sentiment was not enough on which to reconstruct the world. It needed not only a change of heart, but also the application of British industrialism. The rising population needed physical means of progress and support before it could be assimilated into society, and a new form of government was not itself to be the remedy of social evil. Only in America did the boundless opportunities of unlimited space create the circumstances favourable to success, and Europe had to wait for the spread of industry to find an adequate solution of her economic problems. But the democratic leaders did not see that, nor even did they contrive to make use of such material as lay to hand: they allowed themselves to be carried away in imaginative contemplation of magic catchwords. Their theories of the "Rights of Man" proved to be nothing else than propaganda, and social and political understanding did not arise from the simple expedient of downing authority. A sense of man's duties as well as his rights was essential to the successful development of society, and only a genuine spirit of compromise could have brought a solution for the problems of the French revolutionaries. Girondist impotence to inaugurate the golden age thence led straight to disillusionment, and their discomfiture was the opportunity of their extremist opponents. The failure of principle would be rectified by the use of force, and what could not be produced at home would be extorted abroad. A military adventure ensued which frightened and appalled the watching world.

For what followed, then, the democrats themselves were not without their share of blame. They had proved themselves no more competent to ensure the welfare of the State than the old monarchical governments, and their emancipation had only let loose the nationalist flood of the First Empire. They disregarded the first principles of human government, displayed an intolerance that was fraught with the utmost menace, and surrendered to the lowest passions and prejudices in a way that killed all the prospects of consistent action or a firm allegiance. The fault lay "not in their stars but in themselves that they were underlings", and the malady that afflicted rich, afflicted poor alike.

4

In Rome we found that this prevailing sickness was the symptom of an incipient materialism. In the late 18th century and early 19th century the case was the same again. The upper classes were seeking to retain their authority, not for the sake of any ideal of the common good, which their government had long since ceased to envisage, but simply to preserve those privileges and properties which assured them their state of affluence. Like the Senatorial order before them, they looked no farther than the boundaries of their own magnificent estates, and studied only their own material comfort, regardless of a world of pain. The masses of the people, too, from a position of impoverishment and illiteracy, sought their own material betterment to the exclusion of all else, and civilization grew to mean, for them, material progress only. Wealth and poverty tended to the same result.

Nor did the coming of industrialism bring any improvement, however fully it provided a potential solution. For the opportunity that it gave for the accumulation of capital under the prevailing conditions of government merely added a spur to the acquisitive element in men and concentrated their attention more than ever on the pursuit of material interests. On the one side, a new aristocracy of commerce and industry arose, who thrived on the new inventions and rivalled in opulence the old landed proprietors, whilst on the other their miserable employees came to exchange one sort of degradation for another. The materialistic viewpoint was thus only intensified, and the acquisition of money soared from a part-time to a full-time employment for rich and poor alike.

Furthermore, the new industrial and commercial classes

proceeded to launch themselves into large-scale ventures which were openly profiteering, monopolistic and anti-social, and as they prospered in the absence of any restraining legislation, they strove to perpetuate this right to exploit mankind by enforcing on the Government a policy of non-interference in economic and social affairs. *Laissez-faire*, as a political creed, eventually came to dominate the greater part of the 19th century, and was inevitably the parent of immense prosperity. But at the same time it was the true child of materialism. For the moral implications of such capitalistic procedure were completely overlooked, and utility became the one and only value. True, a measure of social progress might be effected because it was expedient and the sentimentalism of the "Rights of Man" was very properly exploded, but economic ruthlessness was hardly affected, and middle-class morality became more and more a matter of convention. In this atmosphere the spirit of social and political collaboration had not a chance to breathe.

5

A complication was that scientific thought was meanwhile disintegrating the whole basis of traditional ethics and changing men's outlook completely. The growing control of the material world encouraged them to believe that all parts of human experience could likewise be expressed in physical terms and that morality along with the objects of physical fact could be reduced to scientific formulæ. By confining themselves to those outward observations of the human mind which could be measured quantitatively, they tended either to dismiss as subjective those which could not be so measured, or to postulate mechanical "explanations" for them which completely overlooked their qualitative value. A habit of mind arose which assumed without thinking that scientific truth was the only truth, and that reality lay in absolute objectivity. Human feelings were thus held to be less real than the external antecedents alleged to be their only causes, and logical coherence and physical accuracy became the only criteria of moral and æsthetic values. Morality, as it had existed before, was either treated with the cynical indifference due to an arbitrary code that could not be enforced, or changed into a science of self-interest that barely disguised its self-seeking; whilst art and, later, literature fell away to languish in the wilderness of theory.

Yet that was not all. Religion, too, as appealing to media

of experience which were not mathematically computable, suffered the same setback, and a literal interpretation of its tenets exposed it to the same irrelevant, but devastating, criticism. The conflict that we saw in the 18th century between religion and science was destined to die away gradually to a desultory rearguard action fought by ignorant fundamentalists, until at last a materialistic viewpoint reigned virtually supreme. The religious backing for morality was thus removed; the spiritual side of man became a thing of ridicule or temporary embarrassment; and any sort of idealism was attacked as imaginative nonsense, since it remained outside the golden circle of real and verifiable fact, by which was conceived only the fact of sight and touch.

Emotional outlet men must have, however, and when the age-long channels were blocked, they steeped themselves in sentiment. Of moral restraint against excess they had none, but only a perverted notion of their own material importance; and temporary bursts of enthusiasm for a sentimental theory in no way counterbalanced the lack of solid communal effort. Personal, material interests stood practically alone, and the outcome was the age of revolution we have just reviewed. It was an open fight between those who wished to retard the progress of human liberty for their own advantage, and those who strove to effect that progress without scruple or reflection, and just as Sulla's legions had won the first round of a similar fight for the reactionary Senate of Rome, so in the Europe of 1848 the carbines of the Holy Alliance stammered out the victory of the *ancien régime* at the end of a turbulent epoch.

CHAPTER XII

"BELLUM CIVILE"

I

WE HAVE now brought our survey of modern industrial society to a stage of development where it corresponds very closely in certain respects with that of Sullan Rome. Both civilizations, despite their growing power and extent, had failed to increase in depth, and the accumulating results of industry and improved organization were being denied to large masses of contributing humanity. The social and political problems of the age, arising out of the excluded sections' demand for a fuller life, had found no solution, and no genuine opportunity was being offered them either for material betterment or cultural progress. Almost exclusively attention was focused on the pursuit of private or sectional interests, and a materialistic conception of morality was blinding men to the need for co-operation and restraint. Competition for aggrandisement was open and unashamed, and for the moment victory in this regular warfare lay with the traditional holders of the Government.

We must now turn back to Rome and discover the consequences of this uncompromising attitude, and see how the bar to natural expansion was to affect the future development of its society. The nobility, through the prowess of its military genius, Sulla, had laid a heavy hand on the prospects of its opponents, and was enjoying the benefits of civilization with happy exclusiveness, even if with a degree of insecurity that was quite unrealized. For when Sulla laid down the special powers with which he had been entrusted to repair the Constitution in 79 B.C., he was firmly of the opinion that he had rehabilitated Senatorial rule for all time: he thought he had given aristocracy the legal backing that had been its main deficiency in the old days and extirpated the very roots of middle- and lower-class opposition. Yet the eight years following his death in 78 B.C. saw the rapid dissolution of the whole imposing edifice and new forces arise which were to bring about the final and complete overthrow of Senatorial government. The re-affirmation of an out-moded system could not provide for the difficulties and dangers of a new and violent age, and political bankruptcy was not to be ended by a mere stroke of the pen.

The decisive reason was that the aristocracy was played out. A strong central government was undoubtedly the crying need of the hour, as Sulla had foreseen, but the Senatorial party was not the one to give it. They could not adapt themselves to the position of supremacy where Sulla's legions had placed them, and they quickly allowed the situation to get as far out of hand as they had done before. Governmental incapacity showed itself on all sides—in the military as well as the political sphere—and still no attempt was made to deal with a social and economic problem that was steadily going from bad to worse. The nobles continued to put their own personal pleasures before the duties that their position of eminence laid upon them, and they were as unfitted for the diligent conduct of affairs by a lack of ability that their training made inevitable, as by a disinclination for hard work which followed from their dissipated mode of life. Their morale had been broken down before: now their vigour was cracking too.

With this feeble power at the helm, therefore, it was not long before the remnants of the opposition parties gathered themselves together and prepared to renew the battle. Their former leaders had been violently cut down in the Sullan purge, but men of ability were not lacking to take their places and to give voice to the common discontent, so that within a couple of years both the middle and lower classes were once again fully constituted political parties, not only with urgent demands on the national body, but also embittered and thirsting for revenge. The political horizon at Rome looked stormy indeed.

The immediate problems of the day were the same as before, but in a much more intensified form—a fiercer demand from the Equites for protection of their vast financial interests, and an angry cry from the Popular party for social redress and security. Both were in no mood for half-measures, and both were determined to make no mistake the next time they had the nobles at their mercy. Any shred of respect they had had left for the tradition and prestige of the Senate had been swept away in the Sullan landslide, and a strict legalism was not likely to prove much of a bar to their fury. For the Senate had now more than ever identified itself with the Constitution, and if the Constitution stood in the way of removing Senatorial obstruction, then the Constitution, too, must go. The requirements of the general public were too pressing to allow lip-service to a despised convention to keep them from their goal when opportunity offered, and passions were too inflamed.

This, then, was the mood of unscrupulousness in which the opposition parties began their attacks on the reconstituted Senatorial Government. There was an atmosphere of tenseness throughout the whole Roman world. Men realized with beating hearts that republican institutions were on their trial, and they watched with foreboding the approach of the impending clash. It was a time of feverish jockeying for position, with men everywhere forced out of the ruts in which habit had ground them. In Italy, and particularly in Rome, the excitement reached boiling point, and the mental and emotional stimulus in every walk of life was prodigious. For when liberty and all that men prized were at stake, and they moved on the elevated stage of life and death, they tapped new springs of energy and walked with the conscious air of supermen, engaged to do or die.

2

We will begin by reviewing briefly the course that events took. After a few preliminary concessions had been extracted by the opposition, the Government gave fresh evidence of its inability to protect life and property. A wild insurrection broke out in the Volturno valley among the most depressed of all classes of society, the semi-barbarian slave-gangs of the industrial magnates, and before many months had passed, over a hundred thousand desperadoes were in arms, pillaging and plundering with impunity. The Government hastily threw in a few raw levies to oppose them, but these were swept away in the torrent, and the way to Rome itself lay open and defenceless. In the capital there was but one man who kept his head, and that was Marcus Licinius Crassus, the wealthiest of the wealthy Equites, a world-wide banker and industrialist, a cool, calculating man of business. He poured out his vast resources and exerted his enormous influence to raise an unofficial army, and after pinning the rebels down till his men were ready, at last utterly destroyed them in 71 B.C. Only a few stragglers escaped northwards, where they ran into a returning army under Pompey the Great and were promptly cut down by his veteran troops.

Pompey's own position at this time was quite irregular. A brilliant young soldier, he had been appointed in a storm of popular enthusiasm to command in Spain over the heads of aristocrats far more eligible and senior, and had held no properly constituted authority. In 71 B.C. he was opportunely returning from a successful campaign by the overland route when he came upon the rebels and, in his own words, "pulled up the roots of insurrection". He and Crassus now joined forces, and keeping their unofficial armies at a handy distance from the city, intimidated the Government into giving them supreme authority. They at once embarked on a programme of legislation which would mitigate the worst of the prevailing discontent, giving the middle classes a share in the administration and broadening the old regulation of food-prices for the poor, which had been suspended by Sulla, into an actual dole of free corn. But of statesman-like reform they did nothing.

Crassus was a financier, responsible, indeed, with his kind for much of the social depression he was affecting to dispel, and interested in no way to remove the supply of cheap labour or elevate the masses to a position of decency and respectability. A stable government and *laissez-faire* were his only aims. And Pompey was merely a soldier, vain, tactless and selfish, anxious to curry favour with all parties so as to gain new commands and new triumphs.

Nor had he long to wait. Government incompetence next brought the very food supply into peril and Rome itself to the verge of starvation. Neglect of the navy had allowed piracy to grow to such proportions that not a merchantman could make the crossing from Africa or Sicily, and even ships of the line lying at the home-port of Ostia were attacked and burnt by the ever bolder pirates. The public cry went up again for Pompey to take command, and being appointed, in little more than three months he accomplished what the Senate had failed to do in forty years. On top of this there followed a Government *débâcle* in the East, where Sulla's slipshod settlement had been violently upset in a fresh outbreak of war, and the aristocratic commanders showed themselves no more capable of finishing things off. Pompey again got the job by popular vote, and speedily fulfilled the highest expectations. Asia Minor and Syria were this time brought securely under Roman rule.

Meanwhile, the political situation at Rome had deteriorated rapidly. The Slave rising of 74 B.C. had completed the ruin of Italian agriculture, and thousands of impoverished farmers and peasants were drifting to the city to swell the already overcrowded populace. Countless well-to-do people had suffered likewise, and borrowing capital from the bankers at exorbitant rates of interest, only got themselves into worse difficulties. Lawlessness increased, and in the face of Government incapacity, radical demands grew louder and louder. More than once the revolution that was ever near the surface threatened to break out, and was only averted by the appearance of two new personalities on the Roman political stage— Marcus Tullius Cicero, the ornament of Latin prose and oratory, and Gaius Julius Cæsar. Both these men stood for something new in Roman history, and both were destined to leave their mark on world development, but their interests were diametrically opposed, and their powers in a world of action were radically unequal. Cicero was bound to fail: Cæsar could only be Cæsar. Their point of contact was that they were the first to see the only cure for Roman ills lay in a strong central government that consulted the interests of all classes in the State. The dominance of one party or the other was not enough, as it did not conduce to that measure of co-operation essential for success, and the present party struggle was a menace because authority was lacking to control it.

Cicero was the first of them to formulate his programme and try to put his theories into practice. He was the spokesman of a new element in Roman society, a growing number of solid, upper middle-class people whose interests lay outside the city in the country-towns of Italy, and who were anxious for a wider conception of government than the partisanship of Roman politics had hitherto allowed. He had higher standards of efficiency in administration, integrity in public life and conscientiousness in private dealings, born of native worth and enhanced by extensive reading, and he aspired to erect a clean and workman-like government on the basis of the substantial body of opinion that he represented. To this he sought to attract the better elements of the old political parties, and thereby to establish a truly National Government that could be guaranteed to look after the best interests of the State as a whole, as well as those of its individual members, from whatever class they came; and it speaks volumes for his energy and his oratory that for a brief two years he succeeded in maintaining an equilibrium of the more responsible sections of the community, which was strong enough to withstand at least one open bid for revolution. But the forces against him in the end were too deep and too powerful, and not least among them was Julius Cæsar.

Cæsar saw, as no one else did in his day, that the real power no longer lay with the political parties, but with the armies of Pompey and the millions of Crassus' money. It was they who in the last resort secured the protection of life and property, as in the Slave rising of 74 B.C., and it was they who facilitated reform, as in the year of their administration. He therefore set himself to create a weapon of his own that would enable him to meet the other two on equal terms and play an equally influential part in Roman life; and to do so, he employed all the resources of his vast ingenuity, all the charms of his immense tact, and all the cool strength of his iron determination. He was a giant among men, and he used them as his pawns with the consummate skill of a born strategist; yet, at the same time, he saw deeper and farther than the men of his day and opened the way to (at least) one sort of solution of their problems. He could be harsh by design, but he was kindly by nature: he was both a brilliant soldier and a master of Latin prose-writing; and he won the unbounded admiration of his friends, the unquenchable love of his women and the mortal fear of his enemies.

From the moment that Cæsar appeared on the political horizon, the scheming of his contemporaries became the helpless jerking of a puppet-show. By calculated pandering to the mob, he rose first to be leader of the Popular party, and with this force behind him created a balance of power with Crassus and Pompey in the "First Triumvirate" which finally overwhelmed the National Government of Cicero and precipitated Roman affairs into the open violence of power politics. Then in a nine years' proconsular command in France and Belgium, adding, as it were, *en passant*, vast new territories to the Roman Dominion, he built up a superb military machine with which, when the moment came in 49 B.C., he swept away the armies of Pompey and the Senate, intimidated the millionaires into humility and allegiance, and quelled the unruly mob to a tense but respectful silence. Cæsar stood alone in a cowed world.

Yet it was a world that nevertheless breathed with relief. The stimulus that had been given to Roman energy by political controversy had now become an irritant of the most exacting kind: physical strength was debilitated by four years' of actual civil war; and nerves were stretched to breaking-point by anxiety and excitement. "Peace at any price" was the cry on every side, and how the victor would exert his autocracy was a matter almost of indifference. In the event, the world would never know what his answer was to be: for hardly had he overcome the last resistance of the Pompeian party than he was assassinated by a group of malcontents within his own staff, and weary mankind awoke to find itself once more flung into the maelstrom of blind war. On the removal of his authority, the old slogans were pumped out again to stir men to political consciousness, but they had ceased to have meaning in a power-driven age, and a fresh series of marches and counter-marches threw up a new alignment of forces in which the "Second Triumvirate" of Antony, Octavian and Lepidus, the new Cæsarean or Imperial party, opposed the reactionary, republican clique of Brutus and Cassius, the murderers of peace. It was war again—war with all its slaughter and destruction, its lying propaganda and counter-propaganda, its cruel alternatives and falsified values, war that no one wanted, but that no one could avert. That was in 43 B.C.

3

Our task must be to discover the reasons for this fatal degeneration of party strife into the hopeless toils of civil war. That voices were not wanting to denounce the way that things were drifting, we have already seen, and towards the end there were few who would not have given anything to avoid it. Yet forces had been set in motion over which the State had no control and which public opinion was powerless to stem; and the armies which were mobilized were not to rest until they had plunged the whole Mediterranean world into disaster. Though wider conceptions of human destiny and Roman worth were forged in the heat of political controversy, they melted again in the flames of primitive emotion, and everything resolved itself into the use of naked force, made terrible and conclusive by the accumulated resources and organizing ability of a great civilization. Why, then, even in the hour that this new and humaner spirit was brought to birth, was it stifled and derided by the very passions it aspired to heal?

The answer lay obviously in the lack of any effective government. There was no authority competent to quell the turbulent elements within the State, and individual sections were allowed to ride roughshod over the laws and constitution. The history of the last century of the Republic is, as we have seen, increasingly that of its most important members, and powerful personalities gradually take the place of the old political parties, giving men new allegiances and new aspirations which the existing constitution was unable to accommodate. It was the logical progression of a policy of individualism. The regardless pursuit of sectional interests had shattered the old balance of party against party until chaos ensued, and the only remedy that had been conceived was more partisanship and more violence, culminating in the Marian massacres and the Sullan proscriptions. Meanwhile, the social results of unlimited individualism were going deeper and wider: vested interests were getting all the more powerful, the masses all the more desperate, and the nobles all the more demoralized; and as the Government's disinclination to interfere grew more pronounced, private enterprise was driven increasingly to make good from its own resources those deficiencies of national endeavour of which it was itself the cause.

Thus, when the Sullan constitution finally displayed itself powerless to defend even hearth and home, the individual was forced to take arms in his own behalf, and private enterprise assumed practically all the duties of normal government. The external accomplishments which followed from this shift of responsibility were indeed dazzling, and the impetus given to human effort by the frank recognition that the rewards of that effort accrued wholly to its maker carried it to heights of achievement that imposed even on the megalomaniac Romans. Pompey's conquests in the East and Cæsar's in the West, for speed and efficiency, completely overshadowed anything that had been done since Alexander the Great: whilst men were stimulated to new cultural pursuits as well, that Romans had hitherto ignored. This was the time of the first beautification of the city, when splendid public buildings were erected at the private cost, of the blossoming of Roman letters, when poetry and prose alike were brought to their fullest perfection, and of the rationalization of Roman thought, when statesmanship, law and philosophy were first articulated and made systematic. It was a time of intense intellectual and æsthetic activity that has immortalized the last days of the Republic.

Yet the sacrifice on the moral side was too great for it to last. For the effects of open competition for authority were cumulative. The success of the few was accomplished at the ever-growing expense of the many, and the greater part of the population was only made more depressed, more worthless and irresponsible, more ready to clutch at passing straws. Moreover, the outward magnificence of the age dulled the better people's sensibilities to the evils in their midst, and less than ever was a consistent policy of lower-class amelioration envisaged by the Government of the day; until at last a situation came about in which unscrupulous seekers after power could rise to notoriety by pandering to the passions of the mob, by offering the immediate alleviation of their want, and by holding out incitements to their insatiate greed. Such men had neither the incentive of vested interests to make them play for stability, nor the vanity which sought merely for fame. They were driven solely by a lust for domination. The fatal defect of immature democracy had shown itself in all its glaring inevitableness, and it was only a matter of time before a master-hand like Cæsar appeared who could win the allegiance of the crowd for initial position, balance the other powers in the land, till he was ready, and then brush them aside with a superior and unlimited use of the same forces by which they had themselves risen into prominence.

4

These were the factors that made for war, and we must now consider more closely why the moves for peace and sanity failed. We have already observed that Cicero in particular had tried to call a halt to the fateful drift, and that he was supported in his appeal by a substantial body of opinion. Over half a century's continuous strife had wearied thinking men of fighting, and intellectual activity had given them a new outlook on the value of human institutions and on the need for co-operation. In effect, it was a demand for a new morality. The old, unquestioning allegiance to home and country had obviously collapsed before the onset of wealth and power, and a broader, more enlightened, but none the less binding one must be found to take its place. Such alone could accommodate the results of material progress and expanding civilization; and such was what Cicero strove to erect by his reading and translation of Plato, by his study and interpretation of Roman history, and by his long and reverent exposition of the ancient Roman virtues.

The problem was his own no less than that of his age. Beneath the vanity, we can read into his own writings that he was as dissatisfied with his own shortcomings as he was with those of his contemporaries, and he found it as difficult to diagnose them in himself as in the world around him. He was convinced of the value of Roman civilization and the necessity for its preservation, and he was likewise convinced that it could be saved only by mutual understanding and collaboration: but he was unable to formulate exactly what he meant by Roman civilization, and he could not find within himself acceptance of the creeds and aims of others. His search was thus a nostalgic hankering after he knew not what, and his stirring call to the nation resolved itself into a vague concoction of resounding words that imposed only for the moment. What Cicero could not do for himself, therefore, there was little hope he could do for a violent age, and the urge for a new code of morals and the blessings of peace had to wait for expression until another war had humbled men's spirits still further and imposed on them the rod of compulsion.

The implications of Cicero's failure will be apparent. We traced in a previous chapter the transformation of the Roman outlook to one of gross materialism, and we saw that the pursuit of purely material interests had become the motivating impulse in every section of society. The conception of endeavour for its own sake or the benefit of their fellow-countrymen had long since vanished from the Romans' minds; nor had they, moreover, ever had any feeling for the inner world of art, literature and philosophy which might have curbed their brutality. They had always been men of action, moved formerly by a tremendous moral impulse which they had combined with extraordinary practical ability, and when the moral impulse left them, as we have seen, they turned to the pursuit of material success for crude and degrading reasons.

At first the habits of the previous code of morals lingered on in part as a legacy not fully comprehended, but the spirit of individualism that materialism engendered stimulated more and more the rise of bold and enterprising thought, until at length morality was recognized for the mere convention it had come to be. This was the moment when men were driven to re-define for themselves the fundamental principles of their lives. For Cæsar the answer was easy. An open and avowed materialist, he had no illusions about either himself or his aims, and he believed only in himself and his own destiny. He was prepared to go to any lengths to promote them, and his restless mind would know no peace till he was lord of the whole earth or he died in making the attempt.

But for Cicero and the normal man of his day the issues were not quite so clear. They realized more and more that a purely materialistic explanation of their world was far from adequate. For their minds experienced, and gave value to, things other than those of the physical universe, and their civilization clearly stood for something more than a degree of material comfort or power. But by training and make-up they were prevented from formulating what those other things were, and could go no farther than perception of the problem. A rationalizing, literal turn of mind, born of their education in a materialist world, wholly incapacitated them from recognizing spiritual values for what they were, and the ancient virtues that they knew from their reading were nothing more than words and phrases that held no reference to the actual world in which they lived. The homely precepts of simple morality they understood indeed, but they had no power to decide where their duty lay in the cruel dilemmas of the age. Creative imagination in the sphere of morals had atrophied from lack of use, and even if they sensed in part the course to which duty called them, they were wanting in ability to divine its implications and the certainty of mind essential for action.

They were thus stranded in a world which had no meaning. The thorough-going materialists at least had the courage of their convictions and the strength of their ambitions to carry them through, and, like Cæsar, strode triumphantly towards their goal; but Cicero and the ordinary, kindly men and women of the age had none of this assurance. Material success had proved for them a broken reed in time of strain and stress, and they had no inner beliefs to which they could turn instead for comfort. They did not know where they stood or for what they should endeavour in the ultimate decisions of their lives, and they could only accept the *fait accompli* with resignation and follow where circumstances carried them. They might seek anodynes, as Cicero did in his writing, or another in his fish-ponds, but sooner or later the times would catch up with them, and then it was kill or be killed. Idealism had decayed until it sought only the Nirvana of forgetfulness.

A better-class opinion which perceived only its own futility was thus wholly without influence on the course of events, and the battle for power went on uninterrupted above it. War was the logical conclusion of a chain of development for which a spirit of materialism was entirely responsible, and the moral idealism that alone could have stopped it was itself a victim of the same concatenation of events.

CHAPTER XIII

WORLD WAR

I

IN THIS chapter we are faced with the task of bringing the story of modern civilization up to the point of development it has reached at the present time. As we realized in the beginning, this is the crux of our whole problem, since upon it depends the correct and clear delineation of the decisive factors which influence us today, and only by seeing the broad features of that story in their entirety are we likely to discern the direction in which they are at present leading. Being so close to the events with which we are concerned and so involved in their repercussions, we are in danger of giving undue emphasis to those which affect us most intimately, and too little to those of perhaps greater ultimate significance which pass us over at the moment.

This, then, is the point at which our previous researches will begin to bear their greatest reward: if the comparison with the ancient world still holds good, we shall be able to use the tendencies we brought to light there to guide us to the main lines of development in the century, 1848–1944: if not, then perhaps we shall discover what new factors exist today to account for the differences. That immense changes in our mode of life have been effected, and that they have brought us into calamity, is obvious, and starting from this broad point of comparison with the Roman world of 80–43 B.C. we will begin our investigation in detail.

2

The bone of contention that had set the world at odds in 1848 had been the demand of countless millions of men for a broadening of the whole basis of their lives. In some cases entire nations had striven to wrest their independence from under the heel of foreign oppression, and in others, liberal and democratic movements had staked everything on throwing off the yoke of their own repressive monarchies. As a general rising, it had failed, and only in England and America of the larger countries was political freedom gradually feeling its way forward. Large areas of Europe remained bound in the fetters of reactionary despotism, and racial, cultural and political expression lay stifled. Nevertheless, the will to break the power of the Holy Alliance and all that it stood for continued like a subterranean flame, growing fiercer as it met the fuel of desperation, and the revolutionaries were in no mood to accept the defeat of 1848 as final. The work of agitation went on.

At the same time, it was slowly changing direction. The Napoleonic Wars had given birth to a new consciousness of national being which was conditioning the development of the various movements and was adding new burdens to the already over-taxed governments. It was this spirit of nationalism that had impelled the Frenchmen of the Revolution to arms in defence of their newly-found liberties and had struck a fire in them sufficient to carry their military prowess over the whole of Europe; and it was only the eventual rise of similar nationalist feeling in Prussia, Spain and Russia, guided by the older and yet deeper patriotism of England, that had at last harried the Frenchmen back within their own borders. The democratic leaders, realizing the importance of this spirit, began to foster it within their own movements, and identified the urge for freedom and independence more and more with the aspirations which centred round national consciousness. By appealing to their followers as Frenchmen, Hungarians, Italians, etc., instead of employing the old slogans of Liberty, Equality and Fraternity, they thus gradually shifted the emphasis in the democratic programmes and sought to depose the old tyrannies in the name no longer of democracy, but of nationalism. The accretion of strength was immediate. Even towards the end of the same year, 1848, a fresh stirring in France dethroned Louis Philippe on grounds of national advantage; a dozen years later Cavour and Garibaldi effected the liberation and unification of Italy under the constitutional monarchy of Piedmont; and in 1866 the old Alliance was finally broken up by the victory of Prussia over Austria.

A new spirit had entered the world. The peoples were each united and inspired by their sense of racial kinship as they had never been before, and they were ready to give their lives and property for the new ideal with a recklessness that dismayed the old aristocratic empires. Their victories were accomplished by force of arms in which all partook; and furthermore, they continued to give themselves the benefit of armed protection ever afterwards; so that by the time the change of government had been securely laid, the new States were in most cases already surrounded by an aura of armed nationalism, and authority was concentrated mainly in the hands of cabinets competent to meet this situation. Nearly all the new Governments thereby gained a military basis, and much of the social purpose was disastrously forgotten that they were originally designed to fulfil. Some of them, indeed, embarked on enlightened programmes of social legislation which justified their inception, and in this way many of the ideas of the French Revolution were re-introduced that have since become commonplaces of social order. State education in particular was undertaken on an increasing scale, as the foundation of successful democracy, and many other countries, including

England, were eventually induced to adopt it. But on the whole progress was slow and impractical, and rarely did it rise above the plane of palliation.

The contrast in other spheres of life was startling. Trade and industry were rocketing ahead, with all the consequences of modern mechanical production—the search for raw materials, the struggle for markets and the accumulation of capital—and as nations changed over to the new methods, they became increasingly involved in their ramifications. England and America were the two countries which participated to the greatest extent in this development, as they started first, controlled the necessary field for expansion, and possessed in the highest degree the enterprise to exploit it, and soon it grew to such dimensions that their national welfare and future progress came to depend on it. Nationalism thence began to invade the world of commerce, too, and a scramble for colonies began all over again as a necessary adjunct of this universal trade. The second British Empire that had grown with the Napoleonic Wars continued to expand until it comprised nearly a quarter of the earth's population, and the United States, by war and purchase, became the occupiers of the whole of the North American continent (except for Canada), and a colonial Power to boot.

The immense success of this imperialistic policy was not without effect on the growing national aspirations in Europe, and in the latter half of the century open bids for aggrandisement were made by both France and Prussia. In France, Louis Napoleon had overthrown the democracy of 1848 and instituted a benevolent autocracy by which he aimed to repeat something of his namesake's glory; and Prussia was a military kingdom that aspired to effect a German union under her own hegemony. The close contact of two such powerful ambitions within the same narrow field made them bound to clash eventually, and war duly came in 1870. Nor did the defeat of France the following year in any way affect French *élan*, which turned overseas for outlet, and the establishment of the German Empire by Bismarck only whetted the Prussian appetite.

Despite this growing interest in military adventure, however, the original demand for social and political progress did not subside. On the contrary, the countries which had adopted industrialism found themselves deeper in the mire of social inequality, as wealth accumulated in few hands, and though the new middle classes intervened decisively in the cause of

108

political enfranchisement in England, and in that of personal sovereignty in America, a policy of *laissez-faire* permitted private enterprise to prey ruthlessly on the masses of the population and bring about a grave state of social unrest and depression; whilst in the less industrialized countries the occasional benefits of social improvement were more than counterbalanced by political impotence, and State interference in the domain of economics and culture, being directed to ends over which the individual had no control, was often violently contested. Internal dissonance was growing no less than external.

In this situation, the Governments of many countries, remembering the access of strength that had come to the old democratic and independence movements from the introduction of the nationalist spirit, intensified their nationalist propaganda and popularized imperialist programmes that they might divert attention from their own organic deficiencies. Whole populations were taught to look for material improvement, not only from their own resources and productivity, but also from warlike conquest and the dispossession of their neighbours, and industrial development and commercial expansion were artificially stimulated to strengthen their powerful demands. State education, too, was directed to the one purpose of inspiring national fervour and acquiring the technical knowledge and appliances requisite for modern war, and a swashbuckling attitude became typical of early 20th-century civilization.

The old Powers, like England, being affected at their most vulnerable spot by this growing competition, and, like Austria, fearing the results of nationalist designs, hastily attempted to set their own houses in order, and strove to meet unity with unity and nationalism with nationalism. In England, the Liberal Administration of 1906 did succeed in mitigating some of the worst effects of economic ruthlessness, and she met the crisis of 1914 with a united front; but in Austria and Russia the provision of a measure of independence to subordinate races and peoples came too late, and they failed to weather the storm. They were merely emboldened to resist.

The result of all this growing nationalism was to imbue the sphere of international politics with a spirit of uncompromising bluster. Governments which had committed themselves at home to programmes of deliberate aggression were in no condition to submit their claims to quiet and reasonable discussion, and threats blown out in the heat of popular passion, whether spontaneous or artificially fostered, had sooner or later to be implemented by force of arms. Opportunities for war abounded in a world of jostling Juntas, and last-minute attempts to avert it were foredoomed to failure. The calamity of 1914–18 was the inevitable outcome of this regardless pursuit of nationalism, and Europe even welcomed it, with minds made light by ignorance of its implications. For an era of unprecedented scientific development had placed mankind in control of forces which threatened his very civilization, and passions were being roused which would use them ruthlessly and recklessly. Yet only after four years of dread and disillusionment did men perceive the error of their ways and begin to sense that the dignity of man prescribed him a better fate. Then at last, in the travail and tears of unrestricted warfare, a new spark was struck which vowed to rid the world of its burden of terror.

Nationalism was the immediate cause of war, but properly directed it was also the bringer of countless blessings. Social and political oppression were the underlying reasons why nationalism had gone astray and rampaged over a world of fair delights, and men saw that social and political oppression must be eradicated before their days would be peaceful. When the holocaust was over, therefore, the main efforts of the Peace-makers were directed to the task of removing the deep-laid causes of unrest. Democracy was encouraged wherever possible, that political expression might be free and unrestricted; and "self-determination" was the universal watchword, that the best in patriotic endeavour might be stimulated. To crown all, a League of Nations was proposed, to mediate in international disputes and introduce some measure of co-ordination in world affairs, and men hoped that they had inaugurated an era of eternal peace wherein they might return once more to their commerce and industry and the private enjoyment of their "brave new world".

From the start, however, the United States and Russia had remained aloof from the experiment, applying themselves to their own individual solutions of the problem, and Japan, Germany and Italy were soon to follow suit. Social and political unrest had found no respite: economic depression quickly made it worse; and a nationalism flared out again that was even more violent than before—a nationalism made more telling, more radical and more widespread by all the advancing powers of physical and psychological science; till at last in 1939, in a hush of horror, the countries of the world found themselves a second time within a generation pitchforked into the ghastliness of universal, total war.

3

It will be apparent that if we substitute individualism for nationalism, the main outline of this story is very similar to that of the Roman age we reviewed in the previous chapter. An insistent demand for social and political redress, meeting only with frustration and repression, turned to unilateral action which used the demand for its own ends, without mitigating it, and led directly to hostilities, culminating in the First World War; and then, though a new social and international consciousness was born, an intensified deployment of the same forces rapidly produced the ruthlessness of a Second World War, from which the results are at the moment unforeseeable. Provided, therefore, we can equate the factors operating in the rise of individualism at Rome with those of modern nationalism, having regard to the differences of time and place, we can allow ourselves to be guided by the events of the remote past in our scrutiny of the present and our consideration of the future.

For this purpose, let us consider again the causes of the nationalistic outburst. The majority populations of the old monarchical States had found a new urge to rise from the position of social and political degradation to which they had been subjected in a former age, and in giving it expression they had grown to consciousness of their common racial affinity. A genuine spirit of patriotism began to infuse their efforts, and many deeds of heroism and devotion illuminate this episode of human progress. Blind and selfish opposition from the ruling Powers served not only to intensify the striving and distress, but also gave the Governments themselves the character of alien and treasonable oppressors; so that the democratic and independence movements were able more and more to assume the rôle of the nations' representatives, and even identify themselves with the nations' interests.

As we have seen, however, in actual fact the movements came to represent the true aims and aspirations of the nations less and less, and in most cases by the time they had overthrown the old constitutions and established themselves in their places, they were committed to a policy of national assertion with a definite military bias, which largely overlooked the socio-political aspect of their origin. Small nuclei which had directed the national effort in the undoubtedly difficult hour of liberation were installed to complete their militarist missions with all the glamour that their victories gave them. It was the old case of a single section of society identifying itself with the idea of the community as a whole, and promoting sectional interests in defence of which the resources of all were employed. And with the progress of journalism and mechanical science those resources were multiplying and strengthening yearly, till at last the picture of a world emerged, bristling with the guns and bayonets of ambitious cliques and backed by all the artificially stimulated ardour of entire populations.

Meanwhile, the same progress of material science and its application to every sphere of life was altering the whole aspect of human relations, as we saw in our discussion of industrialism. Communications were speeding up and economic interdependence was growing more insistent, so that the manifold countries of the world were rapidly developing into a single economic and cultural whole. Though political boundaries were being more and more sharply defined, the ramifications of industry and livelihood were cutting straight across these arbitrary demarcations, and thought, literature and art were being influenced increasingly in the direction of universal standards. Although the term "international" was only coined by Jeremy Bentham in the early 19th century, by the beginning of the 20th internationalism was a fact in innumerable domains of human activity, and was even admitted in many. Civilization was becoming one, and men were being bound by the needs, but at the same time raised by the boon, of a common humanity.

The action of single nations, therefore, in seeking to promote their own individual advantage to the exclusion of all else, by economic discrimination, by political chicanery, and if necessary by force of arms, was not only reactionary and against the trend of events, but also, from the standpoint of civilization as a whole, the rankest and most deadly kind of individualism. It struck to the heart of international co-operation, by which alone material prosperity and cultural progress could be maintained on a universal scale, and gave rise to that competition in territorial expansion and armaments which rendered war inevitable. Even more individualistic and unilateral was this behaviour when we consider that the nations were being impelled into it by oligarchical cabals which used all the resources of modern educational and propagandist facilities to play on the lower passions and prejudices of the populace, and its logical conclusion was, of course, the rise of a spate of dictators in the 20th century, whose openly avowed intention it was to sum up the nations' destinies in themselves. The parallel to Cæsar was complete.

4

Nationalism and individualism are thus two aspects of the same thing, and individualism had indeed been the keynote of 19th-century development. In England and America the Victorian era saw the heyday of private enterprise, and private trading for profit had a practically uncontested field. Its achievements, too, were as far-reaching as its opportunities. It was responsible for the Industrial Revolution and all that that implied; it was instrumental in spreading the results of mechanical invention over the whole world; and individual humanitarians were the sole authors of such alleviations of its worst effects as had been contemplated. But not only that. Matters of civic, national and even international importance were left to its resources, until, in a system of open competition and survival of the fittest, small groups of private individuals came to control virtually the whole food and labour supplies of the world, and thereby its living conditions as well.

The results of capitalism on this huge scale for 19th-century civilization we have already considered. Social welfare progressed only so far as expediency and sporadic humanitarianism could extract from a grudging self-assertiveness, and despite the accumulating wealth and productivity, the mass of mankind remained sunk in a state of poverty and inarticulate dreariness. It satisfied neither their outward material nor their inner emotional aspirations. There was a perpetual, heaving, dark and uncharted undercurrent of hate throughout society which occasionally broke surface on the placid sea of prosperity and threatened to engulf the less full-bottomed ships of State. It was for the most part a latent energy that was storing up unconsidered, but it was one day bound to explode.

This was the cue for the nationalist leaders. They gave their peoples labour and subsistence in new industries that more wealth and more power might be manufactured; they gave them emotional outlet in the enthusiasm of national aggrandisement; and they whipped up their passions with the rolling of drums and the rattling of sabres. The immediate improvement in morale was unbounded. The sense of corporate endeavour they received filled men with a self-righteousness and moral impulse which made them spare neither life nor limb in the furtherance of the national aims, and the visible signs of material advance that at once appeared seemed to justify their bitterest effort. The achievements of white and yellow men alike, under the ægis of nationalism, were quite unprecedented in history, and completed the industrialization that private enterprise had begun. Yet they led to war. For they overlooked the ever-growing fact that the world and mankind had become a single unit, and that political theory was lagging far behind the economic and cultural actuality. The pursuit of nationalism was the pursuit of sectional, individual interests to the detriment of others, and unrestrained competition could only end in war.

5

Having thus established the psychological similarity of the ancient and modern attitudes that led to war, we may now go on to consider the origin of the growing feeling against war, and why this failed to avert it. That men found individualism inadequate as a principle of life, there were increasing signs. Nationalism itself had been in part a revolt against a system of private enterprise that subjected populations wholesale to the limitless designs of financiers and monopolists; and it had already diverted industry and commerce to the aims of militarist assertion. But it also gave them that corporate ideal or sense of shared enjoyment which satisfies a deeper aspiration in human make-up, and without which the greater part of mankind finds personal success a delusion in the end. Patriotism was often and for long a genuine motive in modern civilization, and coloured the drab history of war no less than the brighter pages of peace: but it tended ever to deteriorate into jingoism and elevate purely sectional interests; so that more and more people began to aspire after a larger and more durable ideal. They wanted something for which they might struggle and endure, that would be for the benefit of themselves and their fellow-men, but would not at the same time lead to the violence and unscrupulousness of war. They wanted the enthusiasm of the nationalist without his aggressiveness, the self-sacrifice of the patriot without his cruel necessity. Once more it was a demand for a new morality.

Humanitarianism and philanthropical creeds thereupon developed on the one side, scientific deterministic theories on the other. Socialism, Marxism, Evolutionism, Survivalism and a host of other "isms" began to spring up in the world of before 1914, each with its own coterie of enthusiasts; and though, like Cicero's incursions into the realm of philosophy two thousand years earlier, they paled at first before the vigour and attractiveness of nationalism and were powerless to stem the tide, nevertheless, by the time the catastrophe was over, practically all men's eyes had been opened to the dangers in which they stood, and a determined effort was made to rectify the errors of the past. War was felt to be, not just a calamity, but a crime against mankind, and an attempt was made to assert the unity of the new world by the creation of a central authority in the shape of the League of Nations. There was also a new feeling that the fundamental causes of war were social, and more and more widely the work of lower-class amelioration was begun in order to remedy the defects. Moreover, a collectivist outlook appeared not only in international politics, but also in national economy, and whole countries like Russia changed overnight from a capitalist to a communist basis of society. Clearly a genuine effort was being made. Our task must be to discover, then, why the reality of a central authority did not materialize, why socialism failed to convince most of those whom it was designed to advantage, and why nationalism again over-rode all finer feelings and aspirations with its lower but more tangible objectives.

After our investigations into the similar situation at Rome and our previous study of modern mentality, we need seek no farther for the reason for this failure than in the prevalent materialism. It was the legacy of a century of such outlook. We have already recorded in an earlier chapter how rationalism, science and mechanical advance had led to the neglect of spiritual values, and we have seen that the general run of mankind in Europe and America had come to be motivated solely by the pursuit of material advantage. The feeling for morality as an absolute code sanctioned and imposed by an authority higher than conscious will was withering, and men sought to interpret its promptings by the purely mechanical apparatus of physical cause and effect. If happiness was construed to consist in freedom of expression, that expression, they held, was purely physical in origin, and material comfort and the pleasures emanating from the five senses were its only modes. Art and literature wallowed in the same misconception, and whilst realism on the one side gave itself standards of photographic accuracy which dispensed with the need for creative imagination, blatant sentimentality on the other pandered to the senses of a world that looked only for physical titillation.

Such an attitude had brought its own reward. The pursuit of material interests unattended by any saving moralism had degenerated into open competition for power and wealth, and first individuals and then groups of individuals, backed by the immense resources which this calculated search had placed at their command, had flung themselves into a mad scramble that recognized no law. What was worse, entire nations had rallied to their lead and devoted all the emotion which had formerly belonged to patriotic endeavour to the cause of national aggrandisement, and a rabid nationalism resulted among the masses which was itself but another form of sentimentality. For it was emotion about a half-truth, an over-ripe enthusiasm for an ideal that was quickly growing out of date, and the glowing ardour of their search for glory signified only brutal aggression, doomed to stultification in the blood and tears of war, since it looked no farther than power and wealth.

Now, in the last resort it was the masses that set the pace; for the leaders were nothing without their conscripts and their munition-workers, and the exigencies of industrial society had placed them in a dominating position from which they decided the general complexion of their government, even without democratic institutions. Yet voluntarily and cheerfully they chose the way of nationalism, and followed it with all the energy that their new-found consciousness had roused in them. The slums, the poverty, the degradation and illiteracy to which the 19th-century system of capitalism and oligarchical government had condemned them denied the birth of any feeling higher than the immediate satisfaction of their senses, and their inhibited emotion as inevitably displayed itself in cheap sentimentalism as it was bound to provide the tinder for unscrupulous seekers after power. This was the price that was paid for obstructing the natural development of society and for blocking its natural access to advancement in the ever-present, all-consuming scramble for wealth.

That the material betterment of myriads of human beings was essential, therefore, was obvious. They had to be assisted to a more responsible viewpoint from which they could decide more adequately the true aims of their national endeavour, and they must be allowed to obtain a standard of living which would inspire them with a nobler sense of human dignity.

They had to be elevated socially, financially and morally. Yet the remedies that were conceived were tainted with the same virus as the disease. New creeds, new theories and new ideals abounded in the 20th century, and all were incomplete, inconclusive and unsatisfying. Their basis was uncompromisingly materialistic, and they ignored the spiritual part of experience no less than the conditions they sought to improve. They confounded the idea of material progress with that of human happiness, and by a logical step made material progress both the means and the end of their endeavour. They overlooked the fact that social excellence is not in itself happiness, but merely provides the requisite conditions for the fuller play of all the parts of human make-up, and that material comfort merely accommodates the half of those parts.

The social reformers, therefore, fell into a two-fold error. In the first place, they concentrated wholly on the material aspect of life, which was only driving the root of the trouble deeper; and in the second, they implicitly made happiness the direct aim of their endeavours, not realizing that the attainment of happiness lies outside the realm of conscious control. Human happiness is not to be effected by the simple process of looking for it, but is the epiphenomenon of complete preoccupation with some other pursuit, and comes to us when our self-consciousness has been absorbed elsewhere. Unwarranted implications were thus foisted on to the idea of material betterment which this very action rendered it powerless to fulfil, and from the start they defeated their own object.

Furthermore, every objective that we set before ourselves must have some justifiable reason for claiming our allegiance, and even an intensive belief in the value of human happiness is inadequate by itself. It has no absolute meaning without reference to some deeper and ulterior motive, and will not evoke our direst and unsparing effort without some final justification of its own. Belief must be backed by some spiritual impulse as well if it is to be transformed into effective action—the Platonic problem in a new guise—and as such it can only come from purposes beyond the conscious will. Purely materialistic conceptions like Socialism, Marxism or Naturalism, therefore, whilst able to convince the intellect, had no power at all to fire the imagination or strike an inextinguishable enthusiasm in the hearts of men; and though attempts were made to imbue them with all the mystical paraphernalia of pseudo-religions, nevertheless, possessing in

117

themselves no revelation of absolute values, they failed to provide that intimation of the ultimate which is essential for religious faith. They thus merely devolved into alternative methods for effecting personal material advancement for which capitalism and totalitarianism were more adequately equipped, and even as moves for social progress they failed.

Whilst millions in the Western democracies, therefore, pursued their own individual efforts to help themselves, or fell into a cynical apathy, other millions in Italy, Germany and Japan reverted to the previous nationalism and sought to attain completion in the glow and plunder of conquest. Only in Russia did Marxism make any progress, because there the industrial development with which it was combined fulfilled the crying need of a population that still existed under 18th-century conditions, and the Soviets entered upon mechanical revolution collectively with all the vigour and enthusiasm that an earlier generation had contributed elsewhere individually.

There was thus no basis for co-operation in international affairs, and the lack of it in economics led to world-wide depression: unilateral action to avert it only aggravated the growing nationalism; and at length the last shreds of morality were swept away in the final rush to war. Once again it was the primitive incentive—kill or be killed—and there we stand today.

CHAPTER XIV

THE ROMAN EMPIRE

I

WE ARE now in a position to maintain that there are conceptual points of similarity between the developments of ancient and modern civilizations, and in particular that the present stage of our own corresponds in certain important respects with that of the Roman world immediately after the assassination of Julius Cæsar. The psychological and emotional forces at work are the same in both cases, and both ages were landed by them in the same unwanted calamity of war. We have also uncovered the meaning of these forces and the direction in which they tend, and so we are equipped to undertake the final stage of our study, and by a scrutiny of the later progress of Græco-Roman civilization, estimate the possibilities that our own may hold in store for us. In this chapter, therefore, we will review briefly the events that followed from the war of 43 B.C., consider how far they were caused by what had gone before, and see the effects they had on the Roman world as a whole. We can then conclude by discussing the result of similar activities today.

2

The war of 43 B.C. was quite short. Although the whole Roman world seemed divided against itself into factions of East and West, the veterans of Cæsar stood firmly by Cæsar's ostensible successors, and they were more than a match for the hasty levies of Brutus and Cassius, despite the fact that they had the whole Eastern Mediterranean to draw on. The main republican army soon met its fate on the field of Philippi in Thrace, and the Second Triumvirate or Cæsarian party was left in supreme control of everything. They at once began to apportion out the world between themselves, each taking a separate sphere of influence—Octavian the West and North, Antony the East, and Lepidus, the weakest of the three, Italy and later Tunis—and the entire official armies of the Roman world were retained under their united command. A few reactionary groups still held out up and down the Mediterranean, but they were little more than pirates and outlaws, and their elimination was only a matter of time.

Meanwhile at Rome the shadow of the old constitution persisted, going through all the motions of electing officials, conducting business of State and claiming to order the government of an empire; but it was only a hollow mockery. The real power lay with the Triumvirate through its possession of the legions, and the nominal Government merely carried out their wishes and instructions in everything that mattered. Theoretically, the Roman State was still a democracy, giving equality of opportunity to every citizen, and the Senate was still the main advisory body, directing the counsels of the legislative assembly and supervising the executive and fighting services; but in fact control of the army had become divorced from the State, and the military commanders who held its allegiance were more powerful than the State whose representatives officially they were.

The situation thus resolved itself into a more blatant form

of the same power-politics that had led to the First Civil War. Three individuals had parcelled out the world amongst themselves, and by naked force imposed their will on all within their spheres of influence; and being openly motivated by the one desire to keep and wield their power for their own pleasure, they permitted no activity that did not conduce to the personal and sectional interests of the Triumvirate. All independent political expression was barred, and men could only turn to the thankless task of repairing some of the ravages in their private fortunes so far as the unpromising situation allowed. That they were weary of war and wanted nothing better than to get on with their own affairs, was understandable; that they had lost the ability to do more, was inevitable. They had henceforth to be contented with the lot their military masters gave them.

The whole aspect of life, therefore, now turned on the fortunes of the Three, and it is they whom we must follow for an account of the subsequent history. Their legions were placed strategically throughout the areas under their control, and they settled down at once to secure and enjoy the first-fruits of their victory; but neither peace nor prosperity would materialize, and wars and rumours of wars were as prevalent as ever. The arbitrary division of the world into three geographical compartments was hopelessly unnatural, and outraged a unity whose parts were inextricably inter-related in all the aspects of political, economic and cultural organization, so that trade, finance, the food supply and even frontier security were dislocated and endangered, and an ominous lack of sympathy began to appear between the peoples of the various parts.

Moreover, the balance of power within the Triumvirate itself was precarious from the start, and each of the Three was bound to be sensitive to every accretion of strength that tended to upset it. Meetings between them were frequent for the discussion of outstanding problems and in the strenuous endeavour to remove the causes of trouble, and the results of their labours were embodied in treaties which published to the world their close co-operation and grasp of the situation. Yet still a settlement remained elusive, and instead of improving, the disharmony grew worse.

At last, in 36 B.C., Lepidus felt emboldened to make open demands on Octavian, and prepared to back them by force of arms, but his army disintegrated, and he was compelled to surrender unconditionally to his opponent. Octavian was thus left master of Italy and the whole of the Western Mediterranean, and all semblance of a balance of power was gone. It was now clearly a straight duel for supremacy. As Antony, however, had thrown away his best chances in dalliance with Cleopatra, the issue could not be long in doubt. The war that broke out early in 31 B.C. was decided the following September at the battle of Actium, and Antony and Cleopatra both committed suicide the next year. The Roman world had found a sole ruler in the great-nephew of Julius Cæsar, himself the herald of autocracy, and henceforward it was the personal property of a single man.

This was indeed the only possible outcome for a world that relied on balance of power for stability. In the rapid process of change, the balance could not hold indefinitely, and where there was no other basis for an understanding, the lesser Powers were bound to be swallowed by the greater. Furthermore, no solution could be successful that had for its fundamental principle the disruption of world unity, and the creation of three arbitrary divisions could not hope to be more than a temporary expedient. That the means of unification was that of autocracy rather than some form of federation, was also the legacy of the previous decline. For from the time of Cæsar's first emergence as head of the Popular party, the more responsible elements of public opinion had ceased to wield any salutary pressure on the progress of events, and supreme power had become a thing to be won or lost by propaganda and force of arms. To the man in the street, the alternative was merely that of choosing the winning side for the better protection of his life and property, and any question of justice was settled by the arbitrament of the principle "Might is Right". Politics functioned only in their grotesque continuation—war—and social advancement had reached its ultimate degree of competitiveness—"Every man for himself". Autocracy or anarchy was the only alternative.

3

The reasons and significance of this state of affairs need not detain us, as it was but the logical development of the same factors that had led to the dictatorship of Julius Cæsar, and we have already considered that in a previous chapter. What does interest us is the solution that Octavian worked out for it in a long lifetime such as was denied to his great-uncle. Octavian, or Augustus Cæsar as he now called himself, was a statesman of the highest rank, however unprepossessing he may have been as a man, and he laid the foundations and built the framework of a system of world order that lasted for four hundred years. To discover the secret of this momentous achievement is our first requirement; to find out why it collapsed in the end is our second; and an analysis of his statesmanship will help us to do both.

His first and foremost accomplishment was that he provided the Roman world with the strong central Government that it had lacked for over a century. He embodied in himself the main functions of State, and made allegiance and responsibility due directly to his own person, so that he could keep close contact with, and control over, everything of importance that occurred. Thus he retained supreme command of all the armed forces, thereby overcoming that fatal divorce of State and authority which the spirit of private enterprise had brought about to the detriment of all, and at the same time he gave himself a dominating position in civil affairs, so that he could put an end to turbulence in party politics and prevent the rise of demagogues and reactionaries such as had been the symptom of the previous anarchy. He likewise, from his centralized position, introduced a proper co-ordination into the business of frontier policy, provincial government and imperial finance, and assumed for himself alone the right to declare and conduct war. From his time onward to the collapse of the Western Empire, the Emperor and State were one, and the performance of State duties was in reality little more than the execution of the Emperor's personal commands.

Augustus realized, however, that over-riding authority was only the first step. Peace must itself be made desirable, or in the long run repression would not achieve it, and for this purpose the causes of the previous unrest must also be eradicated. He therefore applied himself seriously to the task of treating the main social defects of his time, so that the incentive as well as the ability to upset the *status quo* might be removed, and the success that attended his efforts bears witness to the depths of his psychological insight. His method was to do as little violence as possible to the old-established forms and usages of the past, whilst at the same time infusing new life into them and adapting them to the needs of the present. The outward aspect of republican government and the reality of capitalistic life were retained almost intact, and his own stronghold of authority was built into their framework as unobtrusively as possible.

Thus the Senatorial order remained the highest and most influential class within society, except for the immediate family circle of the Emperor, but as the old nobility had been sadly depleted by the slaughter of the Civil Wars, their ranks were henceforth opened up judiciously to men of wealth and ability who had won the Emperor's commendation. These men filled the highest offices of State, though owing their responsibility personally to the Emperor instead of to the Senate, and the latter retained, if less and less usefully, its original status of a purely advisory committee, composed of experienced public officials and ministers. The aristocracy were in this way confirmed in their position of privilege and given a responsible function within the new order, but at the same time they were rendered impotent to ruin it by their neglect and self-centredness, and their distinction from the Equites was purely formal.

The middle classes, indeed, Augustus made to be the backbone of the Empire. They were already the main capital-holders and economic organizers of society, and he made them its main source of administrators and civil servants as well. Most of the officers for the army and much of the "personnel" of home and provincial government were drawn from their ranks, and exceptional ability was generally re- warded, as we have seen, by elevation to the Senate. Although the posts of the highest importance and responsibility were retained for the nobility, the Equites supplied the rank and file of the normal public services, and they had permanent careers opened to them, particularly in the departments of food, customs and finance. Senatorial exclusiveness was thus broken down, and the growing elements of conscientious and hard-working people were given an honourable place and a genuine prospect in society, if they wished to leave commerce. At the same time, a check was imposed on some of the worst features of capitalist exploitation, and borrowers of money, agriculture and sweated labour were protected by careful legislation.

On the other hand, any semblance of the retention of demo- cratic forms was given up as hopeless. The mass of the population was obviously as unfitted for an influential rôle in the running of the Empire as it was incapable of looking after its own resources, and its ignorance of State management was no less to blame than its fickleness and greed for the rise to power of those unscrupulous demagogues who had caused the anarchy and chaos of the past. It was therefore stripped of all political significance, including such electoral prerogatives as it had formerly possessed, and these were taken over wholly by the Government, which henceforward appointed its own ministers and staffs on grounds more calculated to conduce to the general welfare. No bar, however, was placed to honest endeavour and genuine ability, and individuals were able, by commercial enterprise or other means, to raise themselves to positions of influence and responsibility which permitted their eventual entry into the middle stratum of society, or even, if their birth qualifications allowed, into the Senate itself. These, naturally, were exceptions, and for the general run of poor-class citizens such social climbing was purely visionary. Nevertheless, the chance of their dissatisfaction was spiked at the outset by Augustus, and whilst their total degradation was averted by a liberal extension of the dole, their interest and ample leisure-time were more than taken up by civic amenities and public entertainments on the most extravagant scale. The worthlessness of the city mob would never again trouble the higher workings of the State.

4

For all intents and purposes this was the final politico-social complexion of things in the Imperial City of Rome, the mistress of the Roman Empire, and as the enfranchisement of peoples and provinces spread out over the whole Roman world, they, too, took on, with certain modifications, the same aspect of life and external organization. Outside of Rome, members of the Senatorial order were fewer, and no dole facilities were available for the poverty-stricken, but otherwise every town and city was a microcosm of the capital. London, Paris, Geneva, Palmyra and the rest were satellites of the central "Urbs", and the "Urbs" itself revolved about the majestic figure of the Emperor. Augustus and his successors stood as far above the wealthiest multi-millionaires of the capital as did the millionaires themselves above the painted tribesmen of Britain, and society was a balanced, stratified pyramid standing on the four-square base of peasant labour and urban craftsmanship. Its safety was secured by the legions which manned the frontiers, its smooth running by the intelligent direction of the Imperial Government, and it came as the fulfilment of the wishes and aspirations of millions of strife-weary men and women.

The results of this system for ancient civilization have already been noticed in an earlier chapter. Two centuries of material prosperity ensued, the like of which the world has never seen before or since, and apart from a single Imperial crisis when the decadent house of Augustus gave place to the Flavian Emperors, the internal peace and concord were practically uninterrupted. Wealth and riches abounded; food and employment were plentiful; and the amenities of civilization made life gay and delightful. Rome became a city of gold and marble, brilliant with palaces, public institutions and soaring blocks of tenement-flats, and municipalities everywhere copied its baths, its parks and sports-grounds, its libraries, amphitheatres and essential services. No private house of any pretensions was complete without its imposing collection of *objets d'art*, and interest in scientific theory and discovery became universal. In literature the Augustan Age saw the culmination of a century of development, and great names for long continued to give lustre to Latin letters, whilst architecture reached new heights of engineering skill, and plumbing gave a new savour and attractiveness to certain physiological aspects of life that had hitherto been purely functional easements.

Yet, despite all this outward seeming, despite the pomp and magnificence, it was in reality a slow decay, a gradual running-down of society. By A.D. 180, on the death of Marcus Aurelius, the army had already discovered that it was the veritable maintainer of civilization, the prop of the Emperors and the holder of the ultimate power, and every military commander of note began to aspire to the Imperial Throne as of his own right. A century of civil wars followed of the most devastating character, which smashed all the semblance of material prosperity and dealt such a shattering blow to the Empire's strength that it was never again able to cope adequately with the growing problems of frontier defence. A new start was made for the moment in A.D. 284 with the emergence of a strong man in Diocletian, but only at a cost to human dignity and morale which made the end come in the 5th century A.D. as a blessed relief and a liberation from the toils of a brutal machine. The Roman world was already dead: its burial was overdue.

5

We now have the facts before us, and can consider what was the defect in Augustus' system that doomed it to eventual decay, and also what was the strength that made it such "an unconscionable time a-dying". It will be remembered that in an earlier chapter we recognized that the motivating force behind the spread and intensity of Græco-Roman civilization was the ideal of Roman citizenship which Imperial policy gradually extended over the whole Empire, and that this ideal had supplied a moral purpose which inspired all the peoples of the ancient world with some of Rome's own strength; but we were unable to define fully the ingredients of that ideal until we had traced the factors which went to create it. Those factors have now been elucidated, and so we may attempt to assert what was the constitution of the Roman ideal from the time of Augustus onwards. We will then be able to assess both its value and its shortcomings in the world that Augustus created, and from these discover the reasons both for the successes and the failures.

The most urgent desire of mankind when Augustus came to supremacy was peace, and at the time they were willing to sacrifice anything to obtain it. The strong government that Augustus gave them was practically the unanimous wish of the whole civilized world, and they parted with their political privileges with hardly a misgiving. Unable to work out their own salvation, they were ready to hand over the task to some-one who was competent to do it for them, and they left the direction of their ultimate destinies willingly in the hands of the central Government. Then, with peace assured, they turned to the care of their private fortunes, and the conditions of life wholly favoured their success. Everyone was bent on the same errand; everyone was encouraged by his neighbour's success; and everyone had ample scope with a world at his feet.

It is clear, then, that their ideal consisted first and foremost in material prosperity. Progress as they saw it, was the accumulation of wealth, the multiplication of creature comforts and the rise of splendid buildings; and the Golden Age that their poets sang was a time of leisure and plenty—

"Summers of the snakeless meadow, unlaborious earth and oarless sea".

Art and literature they pursued, indeed, as part of the Greek inheritance, but they were merely pleasant adjuncts that appealed to an æsthetic underside, to their love of indulgence and display.

It was Augustus' feat that he "cashed in" on this general attitude in its beginning and made it the underprop of the Empire. By his crystallization of the great middle classes and their encouragement in every walk of life, he subsidized the growth of capitalistic endeavour; and by his alleviation of the worst distress of the lower classes he made them contented with the lot such a system gave them. In capitalizing their political apathy to make his own position impregnable, he concentrated their attention more than ever on the material achievements they idealized and supplied them with the perfect conditions for their attainment.

At the same time, he set the train in motion by boosting the public morale—though it was already recovering with the cessation of hostilities—and by inspiring it with the confidence that would make it embark on large-scale capital investment. He infused into the entire Roman world the sense that it was working for the good of Græco-Roman civilization as a whole, and this was indeed the foundation of that moral strength which we saw earlier was to bring their efforts to fruition. If material prosperity was their goal, he made it seem that in helping themselves they helped their world to attain it, and there was thus the precarious balance of corporate and individual effort which is essential for human achievement. Their ideal of prosperity embraced their whole world, and it was accordingly universal in extent. Visible manifestation of it was provided by the might and success of Rome itself, personified in the tremendous figure of the Emperor, and Augustus diligently fostered the emotional impulse that gathered round them by all the resources of advertisement and propaganda. A pseudo-religious cult with Rome as its object of worship was instituted everywhere, and later Emperors even allowed themselves to be deified and worshipped in their lifetime that the impulse might be all the stronger.

It is clear, then, that the goal represented by the attainment of Roman citizenship was purely material in make-up. The people of the Empire had unwittingly come to assume that all the processes of the human constitution, both mental and physical, were motivated logically and externally in mechanical fashion, and that material means alone could give them the happiness and contentment which was their natural aim. With this unquestioning faith in the value of material betterment, they accordingly devoted their whole energies to attaining it, and the status of Roman citizenship opened to them the surest means of doing so. It was the door to official preferment, to commercial success and to personal distinction. It gave them legal protection, tax relief and social prerogatives. Of political power or ethical significance it had none, but these were held in contempt anyway, and their need for spiritual expression they satisfied in sentimental conceptions of omnipotent glory which they ceased to remember was mortal.

It was in fact the harvesting-time of materialism. Men's recognition of material values only had made them so neglect the other sides of their natures that they had no power left to see life steadily or whole, but their ardent pursuit of the things they prized had at last brought its reward, and they expressed themselves wholly in terms of worldly success.

6

To the harvest came also, however, the morals of materialism. They had no feeling for the political or ethical integrity of man, and their sense of his dignity reached only so far as his outward respectability. Having made material success their only goal in a capitalist world that made it attainable, they had no urge to use their creative imaginations to the end of political independence or to strive for a change of social order that might further their aims, and if they were thus apathetic towards their own political expression, they could only in time be more so towards that of their fellow-men Any idea of striving for the social betterment of the world around them vanished with the fulfilment of their own desires, and there came to exist only a sort of business morality, which viewed honest dealing and charitable impulse simply for the reputation they brought.

Though this certainly tended to the successful exploiting of their immediate resources—and two centuries of immense prosperity did in fact ensue—it gave no hope of continuance when these were exhausted. This was true not only of their economics, but even more so of their social life. The individual powers of mankind are radically unequal, and without the impulse of some overwhelming enthusiasm the majority of men and women are more ready to drift along quietly in grudging contentment with their lot than to strike out a line for themselves. The Imperial system gave them that contentment of set purpose, and so ultimately robbed them of enthusiasm. By Imperial intention, no means were opened up to them for improving their minds or enlarging their outlook by compulsory education, and gladiatorial combats and wild beast shows were no substitute for genuine cultural inquiry. They lived on automatically in the same rut and employment, and so slowly lost all sense of contributing to the welfare of Rome, and their *ersatz* morale was crushed out of them by the millstones of vested interest and bureaucracy.

Even though sympathy was gone, they had neither the incentive of extreme poverty to make them strive for escape, nor in any case the means of coercing the system, as a calculating Government saw to their feeding and amusement, and in the last resort the army stood in the way of reform.

As material prosperity grew, therefore, there was no corresponding progress in society, nor any of that broadening which is its sign of healthiness. On the contrary, it began to narrow. Wealth accumulated more than ever in the hands of a few, and the organization to which mankind had committed itself became an inhuman machine from which there was no way out. When rise from one class to another stopped completely, the accident of birth became the stroke of Kismet, and the ideal of material success was worthless from the start. Productivity failed; literature and art collapsed utterly; the resourcefulness of man had dried up.

Yet side by side with this development there was a further factor which turned lack of initiative into positive despondency. As Christ had diagnosed as early as the reign of Augustus' immediate successor, "Man shall not live by bread alone", and the pursuit of purely material interests was quickly fatal to the spiritual welfare of the Empire. Even during the years of prosperity, more and more people began to find a part of themselves stifled and voiceless, and the future seemed to stretch out before them in a blank vista of uselessness that would be ended only by death. And yet death they feared.

The writings of this period are among the most pathetic things in the world's literature. The "Meditations" of Marcus Aurelius, for example, illustrate grimly the depths of spiritual degradation to which a kindly heart and a glowing intellect could be brought by the ultimate hopelessness of materialism, and when the Emperor himself, the monarch of all there was to survey, was chained and bowed by the futility of material gain, there was little hope of better for the rest of men. Though the same turning to philosophy and religion occurred that we saw in the Hellenistic Age, there was again the same barrenness and frustration. For not only was the moral impulse that the apparent unity of Imperial endeavour had given soon found to be illusory and baseless, but all the creeds and worships of the time were once more discovered to be either intellectual or emotional anodynes. Only in Christianity did men and women at last begin to obtain a belief that nourished their inmost desires and aspirations—and that it spread so quickly was the measure of the need—but it came too late to repair the ravages of the past, and by the time it was widely accepted, it was in the grip of political and military forces which it was powerless to undo.

The shadow of Augustus lay like a black pall across the ancient world, and the soulless machine that he had created was slowly crushing out the life and vigour from every person it encompassed. It became a grotesque bureaucracy that calculated only in terms of matter and space, and human feelings were ignored with a brutality less than human. The materialistic conception of man as an automaton without spiritual value had reached its ultimate conclusion, and nothing less than a flood of barbarian invasions, to smash and destroy the whole ancient world, would free mankind from the fetters of a degradation they had inevitably forged for themselves.

CHAPTER XV

THE FUTURE

I

IN SEVEN chapters we have traced the broad outline of ancient Græco-Roman civilization. We have seen how at first bold conceptions of human dignity and worth made it strive for perfection in all the activities of body and soul, and performed wonders in art, literature, philosophy and science which have since become part of the world's heritage. We then saw how growing control of the physical universe and undue emphasis on the intellectual aspect of things turned it aside from a full comprehension of man's multiple powers and allowed his material and scientific proficiency to make headway at the expense of his other activities. His morality fared worst of all. As his interest in material things grew, he lost his instinctive respect for the ethical ties which originally facilitated his emergence into a state of civilization, and his neglect of the spiritual side of his nature prevented him substituting any conscious restraints in their place. Wars ensued, until at last men seriously began to ask themselves what was it in the last resort they sought of life. Some looked back to their achievements in the realms of art, literature and philosophy with wistful remembrance, and tried to renew their tarnished glory. Others contemplated the spectacle of free men braving the assaults of tyrants and bearing high their dauntless spirits to the death. But the vast majority prayed only for peace and comfort and the things they could buy with money. Freedom, patriotism, morality and even life itself meant nothing beside the pleasures of the physical universe, and materialism bound them completely. Then at last they had their way, and they saw their ideal of earthly splendour and unfathomable riches come to reality; but in the very hour of attainment outraged human nature rebelled and turned the pride of achievement to listless futility. Moral collapse was speedily followed by material collapse, and the Ancient World became a memory.

Side by side with this drama, we have also traced the development of our own civilization and seen how it runs parallel in certain important respects right up to our own day. In the years between the 15th and 20th centuries, as in the four and a half centuries between 510 B.C. and 43 B.C., we saw a new epoch, which began with all the glowing ardour of man's unfettered exercise of his full powers, and which had reached out to planes of achievement in art and literature that have since become almost visionary, turn increasingly to the things of the intellect and to the hectic pursuit of material power and wealth. Art, literature and morality suffered as they had done before: men's ideals changed, and their methods of attaining them coarsened, until in our own generation we have found ourselves similarly embroiled in two unwanted world wars.

Once again mankind has reached the edge of the precipice where it is driven to decide what are the ultimate things in life for which it is fighting, and why in the last resort it is struggling to survive: in other words, what is its motivating ideal.

2

Our researches have led us to believe that the most powerful incentive in the world today is that of material improvement. For this reason it is pertinent to have in front of us a simple picture illustrating the results of such an ideal in an earlier age. With its guidance, it is not difficult to envisage what this ideal, standing alone and unredeemed, will hold in store for our civilization, and if it so persists, there is no reason to suppose that the course of our history will not continue to approximate to that of ancient times in the future just as it has done in the past.

We may outline it quite briefly. The three great Powers who have emerged victorious from the war will divide up the territories of the globe into three separate spheres of influence, and with the best intentions in the world settle down to the development of their economic possibilities for the benefit of all concerned. Representatives from the British Empire, the United States and Russia will meet regularly for the co-ordination of financial and industrial policy, work for the maintenance of a nice balance of material and political power, and strive whole-heartedly to accommodate the needs of each other so far as their own individual interests allow. Armaments and war potential will be carefully scaled to the exact requirements of geographical conditions, and propaganda and publicity will testify to the unity of purpose and genuine spirit of co-operation that informs the world triad, just as it did those of the Second Triumvirate two thousand years ago.

Yet peace and prosperity will fail to appear. The economic and cultural unity of the world will have been violated by the erection of three political blocks, however large they may be, and free circulation of commerce, industry and ideas will have been sacrificed through the constriction which such a system entails. For inevitably artificial channels will be provided which feed more directly the requirements of the individual members, and uneconomic enterprises will be artificially stimulated to preserve the balance of power. Nevertheless, scientific discovery and capital development will gradually upset this balance, be it ever so diligently watched, and more artificial stimulation will be needed to adjust it. The constriction will thereupon be all the greater. Competition for fresh sources of power will become keener and ultimately more open, and depression will result.

Meanwhile, the deferment of hopes and the failure of golden prospects will cause the first rumbles of dissatisfaction in this world of unlimited ambition, and a growing recourse will evince itself to less scrupulous methods of attaining it. National integrity and national honour will again be called into question, and at last, somewhere, will arise a frank recognition that naked force is the only way out. In the ensuing imbroglio one of the three will disappear, leaving the way open for a straight duel for supremacy between the remaining two.

Again there will be the same attempt at a compromise,

the same specious collaboration and the same jockeying for position; but just as inevitably the situation will deteriorate into the same reliance on physical strength, and World War No. 3 or 4 will eventuate. From this titanic struggle, made more horrible and more devastating by yet new methods and new inventions, one of the original three will emerge, like Augustus, to effect at last that union of the world which must and will be brought about one day, by whatever means.

If Europe's condition after the war of 1914–18 could with truth be described as a failure of nerve, then the spiritual depression of mankind after a third or fourth World War cannot adequately be expressed, and in return for peace and tranquillity they will be ready to sacrifice anything that the conquerors ask. Political ambition will have disappeared; freedom will be a sentimental vision; and human dignity will consist only in obsequiousness and a big bank-balance.

We thus get the picture of a broken world such as confronted Augustus. Nor will its outcome be dissimilar. A single authority with power to over-ride all existing frontiers and divisions, and unhindered by any nationalist prejudices, will be able so to organize the economic potential of the world that a tide of material prosperity will set in, compared with which the Roman Empire will seem beggary. The unlimited provision of capital for the development of completely new areas and the rehabilitation of the old, will uncover vast new sources of wealth which will transform continents; the continued progress of science will multiply the productivity of labour, till working-hours are reduced to a minimum; and the growing speed and capacity of communications will bring the results to all mankind without stint or fear of competition. New crafts and sciences will perform undreamed-of miracles; economic policy will be laid down by experts and carried through by their highly-trained staffs; psychologists will direct the subtle but inescapable propaganda that maintains the international unity; and the ample leisure-time of mankind will be filled with entertainments and competitions on an unprecedented scale. The vast sports-arenas, super cinemas and luxury-hotels of today will be completely overshadowed, both in size and glamour, by the constructions of tomorrow, and houses, people's cars and splendid physique will be within the reach of everyone. Life will be a round of gaiety and plenty.

Yet political integrity will be dead, and moral interest will be dying; art and literature will become crudely

mechanical; and men and women will begin to find materialism unsatisfying to their deeper instincts. They will experience
a need for spiritual expression, but with faculties untrained
and atrophied, they will surrender themselves to sentimental
charlatanries which they cannot distinguish from genuine
articles of faith, and the disillusionment will in time be all the
greater. Initiative will wither; ingenuity will fail; and the
birth-rate will collapse irremediably. As material prosperity
itself slowly ebbs, stringent rationalizing will tighten up the
organization of society to meet the demands of declining
wealth and manpower, and social enslavement and bureaucracy
will spread out side by side to regulate and increase production.
But the strength of society and of the central government will
have vanished, and wars and violence will ensue, to dissipate
the last remnants of decadent civilization, till at length, in
the wilderness from which it came, mankind shall once again
discover for itself a recognition of its natural needs.

3

In some such way the wheel will come full circle, if the
world makes material ends its only pursuit. Materialism
inevitably dulls the sensibilities of mankind and leaves it
victim of those people who see their way clearest to their goal.
For the best intentions in the world, if backed by intellectual
reasons only, lead to calamity in the end, and wars will again
be our portion, with a tinsel world for our offspring, if such
conceptions are allowed to rule our day and generation.

That material betterment is good and desirable in its
own right is self-evident, and that it is necessary also for
the full expression of every human being, likewise so, but
what we have discovered from our scrutiny of history is that
the direct pursuit of it, and of it alone, is not the best means
of attaining it. "That way madness lies", and other methods
must be adopted if we are to assure our future peace and
progress.

At the very outset of this investigation, however, we
analysed roughly what we meant by civilization, and discovered
that material advantage was only half the purpose that it set
itself to serve. We saw that it intended a state of human
society in which its members were organized for their spiritual
as well as their material advantage, and that intellectual,
æsthetic and moral values must necessarily have a place in it.
Thus the mode of life represented by the Roman Empire,
and such as we have found the modern world to be approaching,

is not even the proper aim we have in front of us when we claim to be members of a civilized society. Civilization presupposes what we have found elsewhere to be true, that man has other sides to his nature than those which can be satisfied by the material world alone; and that these psychical elements must have expression no less than the physical. The critical faculties wherewith he chooses his mode of expression may become dull through lack of use, and may even atrophy altogether, so that he is misled into sentimental perversions, but emotional outlet he must and will have, or he ceases to be a human personality.

Our task, therefore, is to find a method of external organization of the world which will accommodate all these demands of human nature. We must avoid over-emphasis of one or the other of them, since that produces an unbalanced form of society which ultimately leads to its own downfall, and we must beware particularly of a pursuit of material progress conducted to the exclusion of all else, since that assures us, as we have seen, of neither happiness nor the physical paradise which is its aim. We want a manner of life which not only secures for every man and woman the benefits of science, industry and economics, but also compels that elevation of spirit which manifests itself in triumphs of art and literature, and not least in deep appreciation of the world around us. Our aim must be a world that engenders peace and prosperity on the one side, and individual happiness on the other.

4

The Roman Empire fulfilled the first part of this requirement as far as has ever been done in recorded history. Let us consider, then, first the strong points of a system which brought the ancient world peace and prosperity for two whole centuries and enabled it to survive for over four. These must obviously be pertinent to our inquiry, since if we can separate them conceptually from the causes of the collapse, the first half of our search is completed. Now, the main contribution Augustus made was to provide the world with a strong central Government which was competent to curb the unruly elements of society and guarantee the maintenance of order and discipline, thereby creating the conditions necessary for peaceful development and rational, unified organization. The second was that he assured continuity of policy, both with the past by his respect for old-established usages, and for the future by his hereditary monarchy, and so prevented neglect of the accumulated wisdom of the ages which is man's surest rock. Thirdly, he established, temporarily at least, that balance of corporate and individual effort which time and again we have observed to conduce to man's highest achievement.

These three things were responsible for the long duration of the Roman dominion, and allowed the ideals men had set before themselves to be brought to fruition, and we may therefore assume they are necessary ingredients of our own solution—a single world authority, a respect for tradition, and a balance of corporate and individual effort. At once, therefore, we may establish as our objective some form of international government which has power to over-rule national sovereignty in matters which concern the progress of mankind as a whole. The world must be regarded as an economic and political unit that requires the co-ordination of policy which only a single over-riding authority can give it, and unilateral action which endangers the peace and prosperity of mankind must be suppressed as soon as it is conceived. At the same time, national prejudices in matters of culture and local organization must be respected as part of the age-old tradition that men have elaborated in conformity with their own racial characteristics and enabling them to contribute usefully and in their own way to the general welfare.

Next, let us consider what is implied by this vague balance of corporate and individual effort. We have seen it in operation on numerous occasions, but so far have merely recorded it without deeper investigation. It means that the conditions of civilization under which people live provide them with an incentive to exert themselves both for their own advantage and for that of their fellow-men. They work for their own personal benefit, and see the rewards of their labour accrue to themselves, but at the same time the direction of their efforts is such that neither the efforts themselves nor their results are adverse to the interests of society. On the contrary, they advance them. A form of society in which individualism is the leading motive tends, as we have seen, to anarchy, whilst out-and-out communism, on the other hand, destroys the personal initiative. A balance of the two is the essential of perfect health and the source of best results.

What, then, are the conditions under which this dual incentive is present? Firstly, for individual initiative, the immediate requirement is that the individual should see the rewards of his labour. It must be frankly recognized that any idea of human beings working solely for the common good for any length of time is sentimental nonsense, and ignores the demands of human dignity no less than the facts of human nature. Mankind will not as a whole exert itself to the utmost for any cause in which it is not intimately or personally concerned, and it patently demands pursuits in which it is interested, both for mental occupation and material advantage. Freedom of expression, therefore, is an absolute pre-requisite of any useful organization. Men must be free to live and work as they feel impelled, and free to enjoy the fruits of their own exertions. Freedom is not just a romantic vision or a sop to human frailty, but a necessity of human welfare.

This, then, reflects on our postulate of a strong international government, and conditions the form that we shall give it. It must not be a dictatorship such as Augustus created, nor yet a single conquering nation which imposes its will on the rest of mankind, but a representative, constitutional Government, freely elected by all the peoples of the world and concerned only to carry out the mandate they shall give it. It will thus be democratic both in form and principle.

Democracy, however, makes certain demands on its members, as we have seen from time to time, which, if they are not complied with, render it liable to deteriorate into anarchy. It requires a high, general level of intellectual attainment, so that the majority who appoint its administrators, and ultimately choose its broad policy, can distinguish between what is genuinely to its advantage and what is not, and so that it can direct the Government to act in a manner most conducive to the welfare of the community as a whole. Universal education is essential in our world-State, and education, moreover, of a special kind. It must not be purely vocational, as that will not give men the ability to participate intelligently in the politics to which they must apply themselves, nor wholly modern either, as that will not give them that respect for the accumulated wisdom of the past which is essential for a wholesome understanding.

Yet education is not the only *sine qua non* of free democracy. We saw that as early as the 5th century B.C. Plato had diagnosed that democratic institutions could only survive if they were conducted with a due sense of the ethical obligations entailed by membership in society, and that respect for minorities, toleration of opposing views and the spirit of compromise could only be imbued by deep social consciousness and feeling for social responsibility. We considered then how this ethical sense could be maintained, and found that moral idealism was the only sure foundation for it. Only if men

137

are actuated emotionally to a conscious and subconscious pursuit of some moral ideal, if they have some mental standard of correct conduct, justice or fair play on which they are enthusiastically moved to model themselves, will they preserve their regard for the rights of others and allow them to continue in existence alongside their own ambition. Only, in other words, under the influence of moral idealism can men be induced to co-operate with their fellow-men for an indefinite period.

We thus find that in searching for a safeguard to individual effort we have arrived at the second part of our inquiry and discovered in the same concept the incentive for corporate effort. We must therefore conclude that moral idealism is the clue to this balance of individual and corporate endeavour, and that external conditions of freedom combined with an internal moral idealism represent the key features of any unified world-State. But not only that. The incentive to strive for such a State and the conditions which will allow its creation will come only as more and more people set before themselves the moral ideal which it represents. Moral idealism is the crying need of society, of the world and of mankind. Its decay under materialistic conceptions has provoked the present crisis of civilization, and without its resurgence the fate of the Roman Empire awaits us. It was the answer to the problems of 5th-century Athens, and it is the answer to our problems today.

5

How, then, may we seek to obtain this precious panacea of our ills? Plato's intellectual idea of transcendental Love, for example, we have seen is not able to accommodate itself to the needs of ordinary men and women, and though it can inspire a Spenser or a Shelley to heights of emotional ecstasy from which they rain down on us their splendid hymns of praise, it is too astrally cold and distant to stir the chords of sympathy in commoner clay. Christianity, again, is an even more powerful source of it, but confronted with a world whose population is not more than one-fifth professing Christians, and that fifth riven with dissensions, it would seem *on the face of it* that we cannot hope for any extensive or immediate success by the mere process of preaching the Gospel. We must leave our valuation of Christianity till we have considered it more deeply in the last chapter.

There is another way, however, which has already been brought to light in the course of our investigations, and that is the practical English way. During our earlier survey of English character, we saw that English practicality had always managed to maintain in front of itself a moral ideal which stimulated it to further effort. The English possessed a mental standard of gentlemanly conduct which evolved with the years, and at all times acted as an incentive to their social ambitions; so that whilst to be accredited and acknowledged as a gentleman was with most of them a more powerful inspiration than any other motive, the characteristics that constituted being a gentleman were always morally idealized beyond their actual attainment. Because they started with a moral purpose, they came to the front rank; and because they always kept it, they stayed there.

We also traced the process by which this ideal developed, watching how it retained the best of ancient tradition and adapted itself to the needs of new conditions, and simultaneously added the fresh outlook and latest demands of their ever-broadening society. For example, in Elizabethan times the old baronial aristocracy which had formerly lorded it in feudal isolation had been moved to abandon its rough, depredatory exclusiveness, and enter into the more urbane and cultured life of the Renaissance; whilst at the same time the new arrivals, the Raleighs, the Sidneys and the Cecils, took over into their own broader view of society the former chivalric ideas of service and loyalty. They modified their personal aspirations by adherence to the traditional ideals of patriotism and justice which had been handed down from a dim antiquity, and there had thus emerged a new moral purpose in the land which sought the welfare of a wider class and included the achievement of a higher mode of living.

Later, too, we saw how even at the height of Victorian individualism a liberal policy had again widened the basis and extent of society, and by opening it to the great middle classes, had effected a revolution in economics, education and manners. This had not only subsidized an unparalleled capitalistic development, but also rallied the new energy firmly behind the national cause. Again an ideal of conduct and conformity had been evolved which, however inadequate it naturally came to be in later days, was admirably suited to the age of its conception, and served to keep alive the moral impulse of the Victorians in a time of world-wide materialism. Convention it may have been to most of them, but at least it was a convention they followed with all the strength of their immense determination, and it survived to carry the English through a period of strife and upheaval which was sufficient to submerge every other nation of a comparable age.

This process was at work through all the length of English history. A moral ideal of service and social responsibility was slowly but surely extended from age to age. It started from the chivalric conceptions of loyalty and mutual assistance between knights and barons, and was broadened in significance to include an ever-increasing circle of their fellow-countrymen. It kept pace steadily and parabolically with the progress of political theory, so that the extremities of violence and revolution were averted for three hunderd years; yet simultaneously it allowed full use to be made of their boundless material opportunities. The old regime always accommodated itself to the purposes of the new, and the new conformed its practice to the old. English society was an ever-expanding sphere that gathered impulse with every fresh expansion.

6

Today we live in an age in which this process is again in particularly vigorous operation. Once more English society is broadening to admit fresh members to its ranks, and the millions of English men and women who found a livelihood and a purpose in the mills of the Industrial Revolution are reaching out for the full enfranchisement that industrialism has brought within their grasp. A new class is being incorporated into the mainstream of English native development, and with it has come a new social consciousness, a new sense of responsibility towards our fellow-men and a new understanding of the obligations of society. Social legislation on an unprecedented scale is giving effect to the changing outlook, and we are, in our own lifetimes, seeing the results of years of constructive development.

Yet at the same time, in the peculiarly English manner, the very newcomers are adapting themselves to the age-old conventions of the race. Every man and woman of them has unconsciously taken over the traditional notions of right conduct and behaviour that have brought the nation to its position of eminence, and the new awareness is being grafted on to the old aspirations and susceptibilities. Every member of the old working-classes has attained not only his own political sovereignty, but also an impulse to live up to the conscious and subconscious ideals embodied in the concept of an English gentleman, and "gentlemen" they mean to become.

The effect is to modify and broaden once more the implications of this conception and give it a significance that is not yet fully clear. But already new Spensers are at work on it. In the last decade and a half the poetic genius of the race has stirred into new activity under the throb and beat of a social renaissance, and our minds are being re-focused to accept a broader view of life. We are seeing again the multiplex nature of human personality, and growing to a wholesome awareness of the needs of man's spirit as well as his flesh; and the traditional bounds of Victorian sensibility, which had become too narrow for a ranging 20th century and had suffered the indignity of "debunking", are being extended to include a wider area of activity.

Out of this surge of creative imagination there is crystallizing a new standard of conduct which at once sums up and idealizes the aspirations of the new order. It is democratic, socialistic and progressive, but it is also individualistic, personal and conservative. It is international, but it is also national. It is a paradox such as England loves, but it is nevertheless intensely practical and intensely human. It conceptualizes the free expression of every man and woman in all the activities of body and soul, and presupposes the material conditions necessary for that expression: no less, it includes a strictly moral purpose, and forges a bond of union which works for the advantage of all mankind. For it is reaching out to embrace not only Englishmen and men of British race, but all the creeds and colours of the Empire, and this ideal of human integrity is rising in the breasts of millions of Asiatics and Africans as well. An immense cross-section of the world's population is being actuated to conform to the same ideal of character, and to imbibe with it the wealth of its moral significance.

Here, then, emerging again in the hour of want, is a fresh impulse of moral idealism which can re-direct the energy of the world. Just as English industrialism provided the material means of its regeneration, so can English idealism supply its spiritual need. English character can exert an influence for the benefit of humanity no less than English ingenuity, and the nation stands ready poised at the psychological moment to deliver it. For a second time in a generation, England has shown the vast reserves of her strength, and used them unsparingly and recklessly in a cause which is also civilization's; the ideals for which she has fought are firmly established and triumphantly justified in all the corners of the Commonwealth; and the spread of the English language has carried an understanding of her viewpoint to every continent and people.

These things will not be in vain. The example of English achievement, of English moral purpose and English sanity will supply victors and vanquished alike with the focus their efforts require, and the harvest will be increasingly rich and fertile of results. English ideals of balanced and wholesome living will smooth the jagged surface of pioneering races and broaden their conceptions of life: "Basic" English will spread farther and farther afield the leaven of her literature; and English practical genius will find the food and nourishment for morale.

So long as Englishmen survive to work and play—and their determination will ensure them outstanding survival—they will surmount the dangers and difficulties of the future as they have done those of the past, and their rejuvenescent art and literature, music and morality will bring them again the same pre-eminence as their arms, their industry and their commerce. They will give a pattern to the world of solid achievement, of true happiness and kindliness of heart, more valuable than all the precept of creed or dogma, and the British Commonwealth of Nations will point the way with all the genuine virtue of success to the method of erecting the free and democratic world-State which is its end.

English idealism is the chief psychological difference between the modern world and the Roman world, and English idealism will prevent it going along the Roman road. The new ideal of conduct which cherishes the things of the spirit as well as things material, which considers the duties of man as well as his rights, and which crosses the frontiers of nations and takes no account of creed or colour, is a fount of justice and right thinking that will carry mankind to new triumphs of achievement. Human dignity and human humility alike will find the prototypes of their completion in the ordinary men and women of our island; and even though fresh trials and tribulations confront us, as they undoubtedly will, yet only in the combating of evil and the moral choice that that presents us can we prove the rightness and the saneness of our cause.

CHAPTER XVI

EPILOGUE

I

So we see the meaning and significance of many of the forces in the world around us, and so, too, we perceive the influence that each of us has upon them. Civilization is merely the mode of expression that the human race has worked out for itself in its eternal search for happiness, and progress is the sum total of the contributions we all of us are making. How we express ourselves in the quietness of our homes, in the bustle of our daily work and in the screeching racket of war, is both the measure and the source of our success, and broad analyses of history only bring us at the last to this unending personal quest. We are striving now to regain the freshness, the enthusiasm and the wholesomeness of "Merrie England". By the manner and degree in which we accomplish it we shall be able to make ourselves happy: and according as we make ourselves happy, by the full employment of our physical and mental powers, by the uninhibited exercise of all our moral, intellectual and æsthetic sensibilities, we shall exert our influence on the course of civilization. If we are true to ourselves as Englishmen, we shall be true to the world and a war-weary mankind.

This survey would be incomplete, however, if no attempt were made to extract from it some indications as to how these things can be made sure of. Time and again in history we see the forces that work for good, twisted and suborned to serve the interests of evil—it is, indeed, one of the most tragic things in life—and the dangers of it happening again in the future grow even greater with the years. For man is possessing himself of powers which put him more and more consciously in control of his own destiny, and he is less and less able to rely on the haphazard action of subconscious and evolutionary forces for his natural advancement. The progress of psychology and biology in particular is placing formidable weapons in the hands of governments which, if they are not properly directed, can render native propensity unable to exert itself against them, and in an age of scientific deployment the methods of science need to be used to our advantage before they are found to have been used against us to our detriment. Scientific knowledge in itself is neither good nor ill, moral nor immoral: it is the action that applies it that has those qualities.

2

An innate moral idealism has been found to contribute most effectively to English development. Obviously, only by fostering that idealism and providing it with the requisite sustenance and environment can it continue to aid us, and so it is essential to understand both what it is and from whence it comes, that it may be duly catered for in our planning for the future.

Following our usual procedure, let us glance at its story. Independent English history began with the arrival of the Anglo-Saxons in the 5th century A.D., and they brought with them, as we have seen, a bent for practicality and action which has characterized the whole of their subsequent development. Then in the 6th century began the conversion of the new settlers to Christianity, and already by 700, in the person of the Venerable Bede, they were making effective contributions to mediæval religion. In the 13th and 14th centuries, however, the independence of their outlook was manifesting itself and drawing them away from the continental tradition. Roger Bacon was perhaps the first to give formal expression to it.

At that time current Christian theology was under the influence of the metaphysic of St. Thomas Aquinas, and of the two supernatural aids to human blessedness and understanding recognized by Christianity—namely, grace and revelation—Thomism laid the greater stress on revelation. It took its stand upon what had been revealed in the Scriptures, and sought the intellectual pleasure of making the known workings of the world fit in theoretically with the divine purpose, as understood from that revelation. It tended to dogmatism and unwatered intellectualism. English theologists, on the other hand, had always leaned rather to the other great classical tradition, that of St. Augustine, which placed particular emphasis on the need for divine grace, and chose to view the revealed purpose as more in the nature of a goal to be attained by specifically human reason and human conduct. In so far as it maintained that this was possible only with the help of divine grace, and that divine grace was to be won only by purity of living, it was a religious rather than a metaphysical conception of Christianity. It assumed that whilst God's blessing was necessary for the successful outcome of any human activity, nevertheless that activity was itself essential for the fulfilment of God's purpose. It was active where Thomism was passive. It was a way of life before it was a theology.

Roger Bacon re-stated the English preference for this viewpoint as against the prevailing Thomism. He was vitally interested in the acquisition of new knowledge, in scientific investigation and in applying its findings to everyday life, and he claimed for human reason the right to make its own headway in the world—provided always it acknowledged that its inspiration came from Heaven and that its accomplishments were turned to uses which accorded with God's purpose for man as set forth in the Gospels. His Christian belief and devotion did thus not come in question, but he showed plainly the English predilection for action. He wanted to demonstrate his belief by the exercise of his own spiritual, moral and intellectual faculties, and he gave expression to the English feeling that God helps those who help themselves.

Christianity in England never lost this flavour, and however far short it may have fallen of its ideal, it never ceased to regard the ideal as something to be lived rather than as something to be contemplated. One aspect, indeed, of the Reformation in England was that it was the demand of the individual for direct acquaintance with the credentials of something that affected his whole life, and though the interpretation of divine teaching altered in the process and still more so later, that was quite an unconscious phenomenon that habit and environment went far to assist. So long as they had one, they always treated their religion with a great deal of respect, if not of understanding, and there grew up an instinctive stigma attaching to a charge of not practising what was preached. It was partly for this reason that religion in England was marred from the Reformation onwards by the rise of multitudinous sects, all dissenting from what they believed was an inconsistency in clerical practice.

The result of this adherence to Augustinian tradition was thus the emphasis that was laid on the moral aspect of Christian doctrine, and though, in Puritan hands, the meaning of moral and immoral took on strange forms which influenced the national outlook for centuries to come, nevertheless, preoccupation with morality was a constant factor even after the 18th century, when it divorced itself from strictly religious feeling.

Broadly, what happened was that the individual aspect

145

of morality became differentiated from the social. The conditions of commerce, industry and thought generally conspired to put a premium on personal endeavour, and the feeling that God helps those who help themselves was unconsciously twisted to admit its meanest implications. Success in this world tended to be regarded as the outward symbol of inward purity, and the sinfulness of the flesh to signify only physical incontinence and commercial dishonesty. The social side of Christian ethics became obscured, and the Christian view of humanity as a brotherhood joined by a common Father was overshadowed by the conception of God as the strict censor of private morals. The whole realm of external relations therefore ceased in the main to hold relevance to religion, and permitted the attitude, unthinkable before, which asked, "What has religion to do with politics or business?"

On top of this there piled up the effects of scientific progress and Biblical criticism, which seemed to knock the whole bottom out of orthodox theology and render both incredible and superfluous the functioning of supernatural grace and revelation. Thus at length even private morality lost much of its religious backing, and in the later 19th century was destined to become little more than a code of arbitrary and unnatural conventions.

These were the conditions for that turning to nationalism and private religions for spiritual expression which we have seen to be a feature of 20th-century civilization, and there is a palpable connection between the growth of materialism and the decay of Christian doctrine. Both the intellectual and moral content of Christian theology had been allowed to lag far behind the rising standard of scientific and philosophical attainment, and the Church failed lamentably to understand either the requirements of the age or the duties of its position. Christianity became almost vestigial, and the moral impulses which had been awakened by the long probation of mediæval and renaissance devotion, lingered on as unaccountable emotions that bordered almost on the quixotic.

3

Today, however, an optimistic belief in "Progress", as the automatic and inevitable outcome of scientific and industrial proficiency, has collapsed before the obvious baselessness of its hopes, and there is a new interest in the moral situation which is inspiring theologians, poets and laity

146

alike. The resurgence of religious poetry is too strong a movement for it to be explained away by the mere accident of war; the Church is feeling its way forward to a revised theology based on progressive revelation which will satisfy the intellectual demand of men for a reasoned metaphysic; and at the same time the conviction is spreading that man needs the strength which the sense of contact with a supra-conscious world alone can bestow. Recent thought has shown a growing tendency to recognize the dependence of morality for sanction on some sort of religious value, and it is becoming increasingly clear that the moral idealism of which the English people are capable is the legacy of the deep religious conviction in former times. Christian ethic, therefore, is being viewed with new eyes, especially after having been neglected for so long, and the social side of its teaching is becoming apparent no less than the private.

But that is not all. The ingenuity of Englishmen is preparing a practical solution for the present *impasse*, which will admit once more of men living the religion to which they have turned, and it will be possible to restore the moral background to just those departments of modern life which for so long have been separated from Christian influence and have brought us into our present danger. Economic and political functions will then be seen in their proper perspectives, and will cease to be the only values in our view of life. We shall see things all-round.

A Christian society is the new revelation. Despite its revealed character, however, there is nothing new about it. It is rather the new consciousness of a perfectly logical viewpoint. For provided we once accept the point of view of the Christian social ethic, it is a truism that industry, commerce and government exist, not for the purpose of exploiting the general public, but to serve it, and that we should look on our whole working life, not from the particular point of view of capital, management or labour, but from that of the community of which we are a part. Fundamentally, the *raison d'être* of industry is to provide goods for the consumer, and there is no moral justification for changing it to one of making the largest possible profits. Financiers, shareholders, accountants and labour are undoubtedly necessary parts of its organization, but they are still incidental to the main purpose, still means to an end. Similarly, the purpose of government is to maintain order and efficient co-ordination of effort, not to consolidate the interests of one particular class, and both

147

laissez-faire and nationalization conflict with this purpose. The purely materialistic outlook, therefore, the profit-motive standing alone, or even foremost, is quite unnatural and illogical; and the concept of Christian society demands that it should be modified—modified without the impersonal methods and stifling effects of nationalization and bureaucracy.

That this can be done in practice, moreover, is becoming increasingly clear. Already various suggestions have been put forward which would conduce to the desired result, and it only remains to put the best of them in operation. For example, the limitation of dividends to a statutory maximum, coupled with legislation covering the disposal of excess profits, the issue of bonus shares, promotion of subsidiary companies, export of capital, etc., would confine the profit-motive to the provision of a fair return on investments, and thereby remove the main mischief-making potentialities of Capital, however unconsidered they may be in most cases. The establishment of a General Industrial Council, to take over many of the functions of the present Board of Trade, and representing equally Capital, Management and Labour, could plan and organize the whole industrial capacity of the country and ensure that private enterprise tended to the common good. The Council would work through specialized committees on the lines of the present manufacturers' associations, but each comprising Trades Union representatives as well, and govern-mental participation would be confined to a few members on the general body to interpret the interests of the consumer. Again, control of the joint-stock banks by the Bank of England would ensure a credit-policy that worked for the benefit of industry and employment, rather than of the shareholders' dividends; whilst in individual public companies the elevation of a member of the local Works' Committee to the board of directors would give the employees that share in the manage-ment which is their present incongruous lack.

Changes of this sort would revolutionize the whole of our attitude towards the business of living, and throw the emphasis in an entirely fresh direction. They would supply the basis for a solution of many of the present apparently insoluble prob-lems, and at the same time do the least possible violence to the established order. Moreover, the belief that they are not impossible of attainment is strengthened by the fact that the trend is already towards them. In other words, they would be a practical answer. For the essence of practicality is that it adapts the given means to new purposes. It is the art of

148

learning by experience and modifying what has stood the test of time so that it will work under changed conditions. It is neither practical nor practicable to scrap one form of society and replace it with another, and only visionaries and sentimentalists can contemplate the abolition of private property by a mere stroke of the pen, or hope to alter the facts of human nature. The things that exist must necessarily be the material of the new edifice, and plans must be laid to suit that material.

And because the material is resistant, and human nature is habit-ridden, it is essential that there should be some community to keep the aims of a Christian society always before us, and never cease to spur us on to greater efforts. The only body competent to play that part is the Church, and that the Church should flourish is thus a matter of national as well as personal importance. Only the Church can give the leadership which will ensure that public morality is based on Christian principles instead of on political expediency, and such leadership can be given only by a Church which has the allegiance of men's hearts and minds. The effect of a small community such as the Church is ideally intended to be, living a religion which wins intellectual approval, implants moral conviction and inspires artistic activity, has always been profound in the extreme, and the ever-present spectacle of men devoting themselves indefatigably to some ideal which has universal respect is the strongest possible incentive in favour of that ideal. Such is the significance of the Church in a Christian society.

4

What the Church can be for our own national life, the British race can be for the world. By setting an example of vigorous and enterprising society run on lines of the strictest justice and equity, the British Commonwealth can exert an incalculable influence on the progress of civilization. If our country is ridden with unemployment, marred by social injustice and racked with industrial dissension, we shall rely solely on brute force to impose our aspirations on the world, and where that leads we have already seen. But if we present the picture of a Christian community, joined successfully for the sole intention of promoting human happiness both at home and abroad, we shall add the inestimable strength of moral suasion to our cause and light a train whose effects can be unending. Force, and even discipline, alone, never in the long run attain their desired effect, but strength backed by an unquestioned rectitude is an irresistible combination.

That the most salient external feature of civilization during the past two centuries has been industrialization is obvious, and it is also becoming obvious that the Industrial Revolution is not to be viewed as a single event completed more than a hundred years ago. It is a living process that began about 1750, that is still active and still holds a long history in front of it. Immense chapters of intensive mechanization and mass-production are still to be written, and many of the social and political problems of our day are really the symptoms of incomplete, or the growing-pains of uneven, development. The reason is that hitherto its progress has been haphazard and unconsidered, and we are realizing that henceforward it must be planned and purposeful. It holds blessings in store for us if it is controlled, but it also promises us the most ghastly horrors if it is not. Yet such control will not be permitted by any other attitude than one that places a unique value on the welfare of every single individual and views the purpose of industry, not solely as a private profit-making device, but rather as a means of efficient service.

For example, one of the direst needs of the moment is shorter working-hours. No one can cultivate or train his finer sensibilities who spends his whole energy in the numbing conditions of modern industry, and no one but a superman can be creative who sears his soul by machine-minding. We desperately need a chance to open our hearts to the benign influence of our own natures and that of the country we live in, so that the things of the spirit may ripen and mature, and the employment of our leisure time rise above the level of modern mechanical amusements. But the increased labour-costs that this entails will only be offset by increased mass-production and rationalization of industry, and only central planning and controlled investment can do that successfully or adequately. We need to mechanize the whole of our national assets with the same immediacy and effectiveness as we mechanized our army in war-time, and only a new attitude and united effort can do it.

Similarly, nothing but a fresh outlook on commerce will bring improvement in our relations with countries overseas. We are dependent on foreign supplies of food and raw materials for our very existence, and this is the whole basis of our participation in world affairs. We have to re-export to live. But so long as we are entirely governed by the profit-motive and manufacturers work independently for their own advantage, we shall be tempted to subsidize our exports by all the artificial stimulants that a warped nationalism invented, and so contribute further to the welter of conflict and misunderstanding that is violating the economic unity of the world. If, on the other hand, the fundamental purpose of our industry is recognized to be that of service, and we frankly acknowledge our dependence on imports, the spirit that will actuate our exporting will be one of genuine gratitude as it is towards our allies in war-time. We shall rely on the planned efficiency of our re-organized methods of production, and this will open markets to us more securely than any subsidies. A concern, too, will be awakened for our foreign purchasers and suppliers which will speedily admit of that same largeness of outlook which turned the second British Empire into a Commonwealth of Nations; and by customs and political unions, first near at hand in Western Europe, and then farther afield, not only will the incentive be created to promote the same conditions of stability and progress abroad that we intend for ourselves at home, but also a practical example will be given to the world of a readiness to limit national sovereignty in favour of international co-operation. Open and unambiguous declarations of our pacific intentions will undoubtedly go far to dispel the suspicions of the other world-Powers, especially if they are backed by an unhesitating willingness to collaborate in international problems; but the clearest indication of our goodwill will be practical measures in the dangerous field of finance and economics. We have a long historical connection with a system of power-politics which must be proved not to implicate us in a desire for its continuance, but only a complete change of attitude towards the commercial aspect of life will indeed take that desire from us.

From whatever point of view it is considered, it is brought home to us that to pursue the moral ideal which a Christian society represents is the only sure foundation for a lasting and prosperous peace. An improvement in human relations will make itself apparent only when each one of us admits his own share of responsibility for past and present contentions, and social and political injustice will be removed only if we begin by rectifying the delinquencies in our own lives and conduct. To do so has always been an English tradition: to do so now is to fill the greatest rôle in history.

For more than a century the British race has travestied that tradition. It has lived in a world of figures and statistics which have ceased to count the value of human life, and bound itself to a system that has stifled the humanity of rich and poor alike. Figures and statistics are obviously imperative, but they are means and not an end. The profit-motive is likewise an inevitable concomitant of commerce and industry, but it does not stand alone. These things exist that human beings may live and work and be happy, not that millions of working people may find a hazardous and bare subsistence; and until the profit-motive is replaced by that of service and the whole direction of our living thereby reorientated, there is no hope that unemployment will diminish, labour problems be solved or social harmony eventuate. But once that is done, once the moral obligations of the ordinary contacts of life are brought home to us, then the planning and co-ordination of effort which alone can effect social improvement will be feasible. We shall be able to live lives of usefulness, dignity and interest. As each one of us attempts to live the principles of Christian society in his own life, as we all admit our own personal responsibility for the crimes of social injustice—for example by drawing dividends from unprincipled companies and actually working for them—we will retain and foster the moral idealism of which we are capable. Then, and then only, will we have the power to carve for ourselves careers that open up all the joys of living, physical, mental and spiritual.

Three things are fundamental to success—the honesty of our politicians, the fearlessness of our Churchmen, and the practical ability of our people. With these three, and the grace of God, we shall become, as far as is given to man . . .

"Good, great and joyous, beautiful and free".